First edition © Macmillan Publishers Limited, 1980
Second edition © Macmillan Publishers Limited, 1985
This edition © Macmillan Publishers Limited, 1987

First published in three volumes. The Prehistoric World, Cold-Blooded Animals, Warm-Blooded Animals, 1980.
This edition published 1987 by
MACMILLAN CHILDREN'S BOOKS
A division of Macmillan Publishers Ltd.
4 Little Essex Street, London WC2R 3LF and Basingstoke companies and representatives throughout the world

British Library Cataloguing in Publishing Data
A New look at animals. – (A New look at series).
1. Animals – Juvenile literature
591   QL49
ISBN 0-333-44869-3
Printed in Hong Kong

Chief Educational Adviser
Lynda Snowdon

Teacher Advisory Panel
Helen Craddock, John Enticknap, Arthur Razzell

Editorial Board
Jan Burgess, Rosemary Canter, Philip M. Clark, Beatrice Phillpotts, Sue Seddon, Philip Steele

Picture Researchers
Caroline Adams, Anne Marie Ehrlich, Gayle Hayter, Ethel Hurwicz, Pat Hodgson, Stella Martin, Frances Middlestorb

Designer
Keith Faulkner

Contributors and consultants
John E. Allen, Neil Ardley, Sue Becklake, Robert Burton, Barry Cox, Jacqueline Dineen, David J. Fletcher, Plantagenet Somerset Fry, Bill Gunston, Robin Kerrod, Mark Lambert, Anne Millard, Kaye Orten, Ian Ridpath, Peter Stephens, Nigel Swann, Aubrey Tulley, Tom Williamson, Thomas Wright

A NEW LOOK AT
ANIMALS

M

Contents

The Prehistoric World

UNDERSTANDING FOSSILS

Long, long ago the world was full of many strange animals. Over millions of years new kinds of life evolved. Other animals died out. We know about animals that have died out because remains of their bodies were left in rocks. These remains are called fossils. Here is one way that an animal can become a fossil.

The animal with plate-like spikes on its back is called Stegosaurus. A meat-eating animal has seen it.

Stegosaurus tries to escape from the meat-eating animal. But Stegosaurus cannot run fast. It runs into a river to escape.

The river is deep, and Stegosaurus drowns. Later its body is left on a mud bank in the river. Its flesh decays. Only its skeleton is left.

In the winter, the water rises. It covers the skeleton of Stegosaurus with a thick coat of mud.

More and more layers of mud cover the skeleton. The mud and the bones of Stegosaurus turn into hard rock.

Over many years the land rises. The wind and rain slowly wear down the rocks from above the skeleton.

Eventually the skeleton has no more rocks covering it. Scientists who study prehistoric animals find it.

The scientists carefully uncover all the bones. They remove the bones and take them to a museum.

In the museum, the scientists take away all the rock from around the bones. Then they put the bones back together. They make a special metal frame to support the skeleton.

Finding fossils

This scientist found the skeleton of a dinosaur in the desert. He used small chisels to remove the rock from the bones. Although the bones were very hard, they were badly broken. They were broken because they had been in the rocks for such a long time. The scientist strengthened the bones with special plastics.

In prehistoric times, there was a deep pool of tar in this place. There was water on the top of the tar. Animals came to drink the water, and stuck in the tar. Here are their bones.

Beaches and cliffs are good places to find fossils. The sea and the rain wear away the rocks, and uncover other rocks. The rocks underneath are very old. They may contain fossils.

Kinds of fossils

Some fossils are the remains of the hard parts of an animal or plant. Other fossils are only the print of its surface. Very occasionally scientists find a complete little animal that has been trapped in the sticky sap of a tree. It takes millions of years to make a real fossil. But you can easily make copies of fossils.

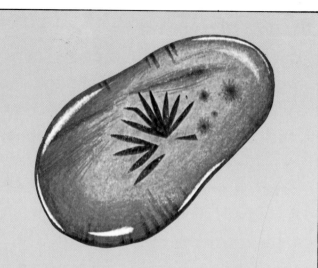

This leaf is preserved in amber. Amber is the sap of trees or plants that has hardened.

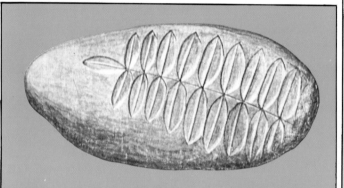

Long ago, a leaf fell into some soft mud. The mud hardened and turned into rock. The leaf print is still clear.

You can embed a leaf in clear resin. First half fill the pot with resin.

You can make your own impressions of a leaf by using soft plasticene.

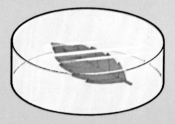

Wait until the resin becomes hard. Then add the leaf and pour the rest of the resin into the pot.

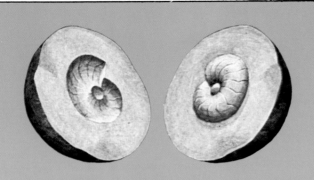

A fossil leaves a hollow or 'mould' in the rock. This can be filled up to give a 'cast' of the fossil.

You can push a shell into soft clay to get a mould of its shape.

Then paint the clay with water. Now you can pour on some plaster.

Peel the clay away from the dry plaster. You can now see the 'cast'.

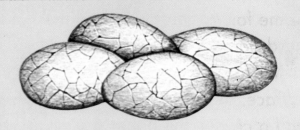

Sometimes we find the fossil eggs of dinosaurs or birds.

You can make your own fossil eggs by using some egg-shaped pebbles.

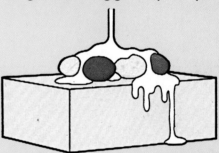

Pour some plaster over the pebbles and leave it until it sets hard.

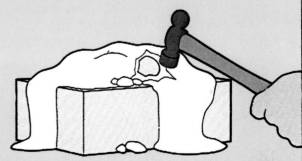

Then carefully chip away some of the plaster. You can see the buried 'eggs'.

What fossils tell us

Sometimes scientists find all the bones of a skeleton connected together. This does not happen very often. Usually they find only a few bones. Often the bones are all jumbled together. You might think that it would be difficult to put all the bones back in the right positions. But really it is easy.

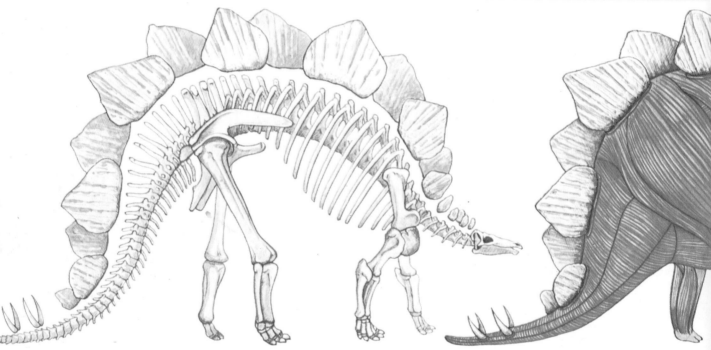

Scientists know that dinosaurs did not have hair or feathers. They know that some dinosaurs had lumps of bone in their skins.

Prints of the skin of dinosaurs show that most dinosaurs had leathery skins. So we can guess what Stegosaurus looked like.

Stegosaurus did not look like this!

Scientists compare the bones they find with the bones of living animals. They can soon tell where each bone belongs. On the bones, scientists can see the marks where the muscles were attached. Then they work out the shape of the body.

Stegosaurus ate plants. It probably had a dull coloured skin, so that meat-eating animals could not see it very easily. Its skin would not have been brightly coloured, but it may have had spots or stripes. Maybe it looked like one of these animals.

EARLY LIFE

The earth probably began as a hot ball of different kinds of gas. Gradually it cooled and became solid. Later still it became cool enough for the steam to turn into water. Only then could living things develop. At first there were only tiny germs. Plants developed later.

gas

plant life begins on land

volcanoes

rain

settled landscape and seas

microscopic pond life

After the plants had appeared, animal life began. Animals eat plants or other animals. They can move.

The first plants and animals were very tiny. They lived in the sea. Larger plants that could live on land developed much later.

Early worms and jellyfish

Scientists divide up the history of the earth into different Periods and give a name to each one. The earliest Period is called the Precambrian. We do not know much about the life of that time. But there are lots of fossils from the next Period. This is called the Cambrian Period.

This is one of the oldest animals we know about. It was a jellyfish. It lived in the Precambrian Period.

This worm lived in the Precambrian Period. When it died a cast of its body was left in the mud of the sea.

corals

giant nautiloids

14

This scene shows the sea life in the
Cambrian Period. This Period came
after the Precambrian Period.
The animals with long bodies and
tentacles are called nautiloids.
Trilobites crawled on the bottom.
Sea urchins lived there too.

jellyfish

sponges

sea
urchins

trilobites

brachiopods

Early sea creatures

Many more millions of years passed by. Here is the life of the Silurian Period, about 400 million years ago. The nautiloids now had curved shells. The animal with pincers is called a eurypterid. It was 2 metres long and ate other animals that lived in the sea.

The trilobites crawled on the bottom of the sea, eating the mud. They could roll up into a ball.

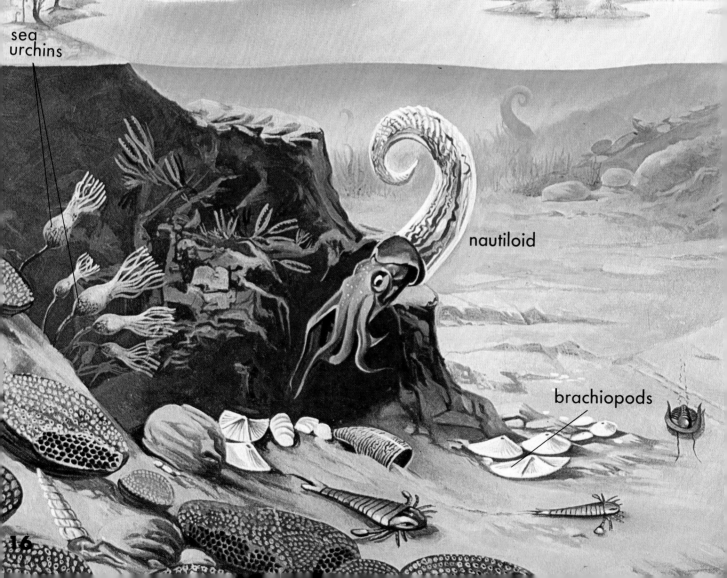

sea urchins

nautiloid

brachiopods

The animals on long stalks which you can see in the picture are called sea-lilies. They gathered tiny specks of food from the sea water. During this time, sea creatures made reefs of hard rock. The rock was formed by their skeletons. Today, coral is made in the same way.

Nautiloids that developed later were called ammonites. They filled their shells with gas to float.

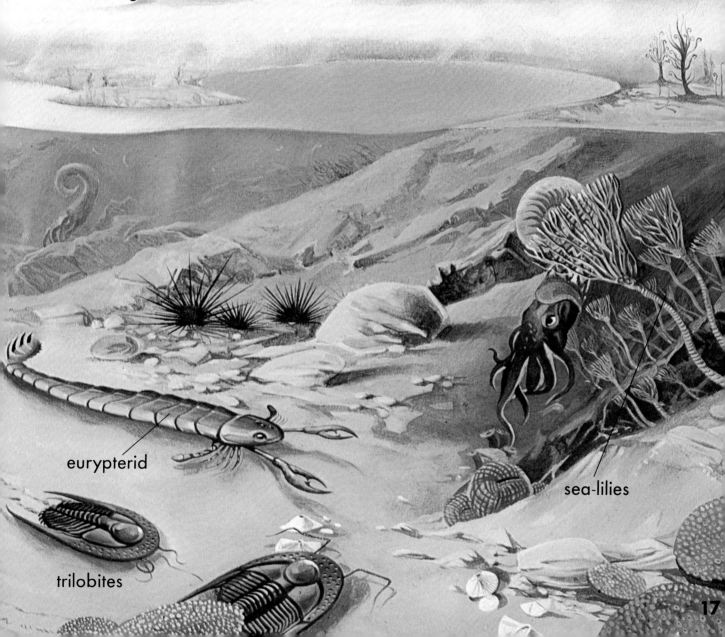

eurypterid

sea-lilies

trilobites

Fish with armour

The first fish evolved in the sea over 400 million years ago. Most of them moved very slowly. They had a thick covering of bone on their heads, and on the front part of their bodies. Behind that, they had thick scales. Some fish, like Drepanaspis and Hemicyclaspis, had flat bodies.

Drepanaspis

Dunkleosteus

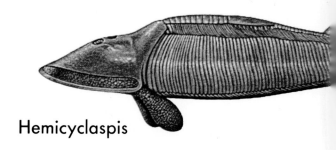

Hemicyclaspis

Pterichthys lived on the bottom of the sea. It pushed itself along with bony flippers. Parexus had several sets of fins and could swim faster. The biggest and most frightening fish was Dunkleosteus. It had strong plates of bone in its large head. These were its 'teeth'. It used them to crunch up the fish that it ate.

Dunkleosteus

Pterichthys

Pteraspis

Parexus

Dunkleosteus was about 9 metres long. It was as long as a bus or a coach. This 7 year old girl would not have reached up to the top of its body. It had powerful fins.

The coelacanth story

The story of the coelacanth is a strange one. Coelacanths were fish with strong muscular fins. Fossils of them have been found in many rocks. But all the rocks they have been found in are at least 65 million years old. Scientists thought that all the coelacanths had died out.

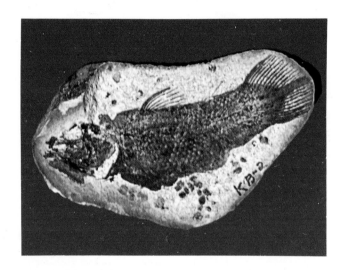

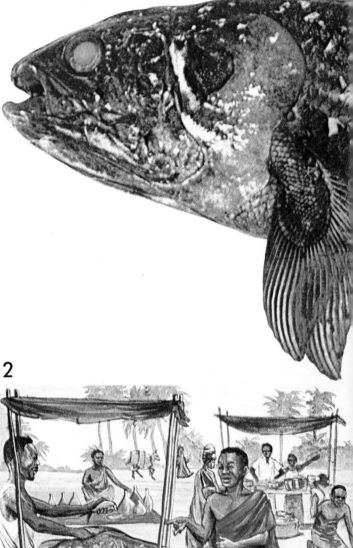

But one day some Africans went fishing. They lived on some islands near Africa. There was a big blue fish among the fish they caught.

2

1

The fish was taken to the market to be sold with the others. But a lady called Miss Latimer noticed that one of the fish was very strange. She sent it to a scientist.

Latimeria is quite a big fish. It is nearly 2 metres long. It has a big head and strong fins. Latimeria lives in deep water. This makes it difficult to catch.

The scientist realized that the strange fish was a coelacanth. It was the first one to be caught and recognized. It was taken to a museum.

4

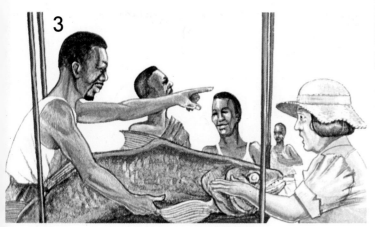

The coelacanth was named Latimeria after the person who took it to the scientist. Now scientists have caught another 50 coelacanths. The fish have been put in museums.

FROM WATER TO LAND

Plants, like animals, found it difficult to live on land. To grow straight, they had to have strong stems. They also had to evolve a waterproof covering so that they did not shrivel up. The pollen of these early plants was carried by the wind. They did not have any flowers like the plants that are alive today.

This is a fossil of the first land plant. It is shown here 12 times bigger than life. It is called Cooksonia.

Today little horsetails grow in marshy places. Millions of years ago plants like these grew into tall trees.

In the big picture you can see some of the early plants.

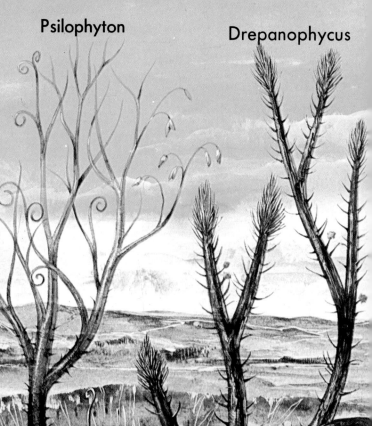

Psilophyton

Drepanophycus

Rhynia

This living plant is called Psilotum.
It looks like the fossil Cooksonia.
It lived in warm, tropical places.

Little clubmosses also grew into
great trees in the first forests.
Protolepidodendron was a
fossil clubmoss.

Protolepidodendron

Archaeopteris

Cyclostigma

23

Early amphibians

Most fish cannot live on land. They cannot breathe air. Their fins are too weak to support their bodies on the ground. But a few fish can wriggle out onto the land, like the little mudskippers in the picture below. Some fish have got lungs. They can breathe air if all the water in the river dries up.

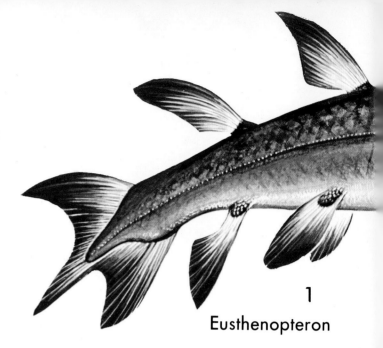

1
Eusthenopteron

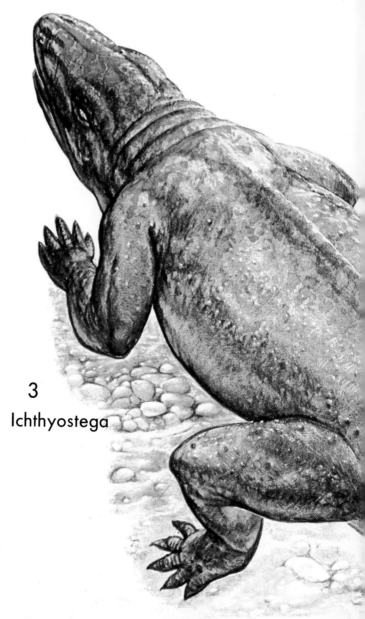

3
Ichthyostega

Amphibians can live in the water or on the land. They use their lungs to breathe air. The first amphibians developed from a fish called Eusthenopteron. This fish had lungs and strong fins. Eusthenopteron came onto land to escape from other fish. It found plenty of worms and snails to eat on land.

The first amphibian that scientists know about is called Ichthyostega. It had quite strong limbs instead of fins. It did not have gills. It breathed air instead of water. There must have been a creature half-way between Eusthenopteron and Ichthyostega. Perhaps it looked like this creature on the right.

2

Early swamp life

The first trees grew about 300 million years ago. This Period is called the Carboniferous Period. The trees grew in the warm parts of the world. Many of the trees grew very tall. They grew up to 40 metres high, and lived in steamy swamps.

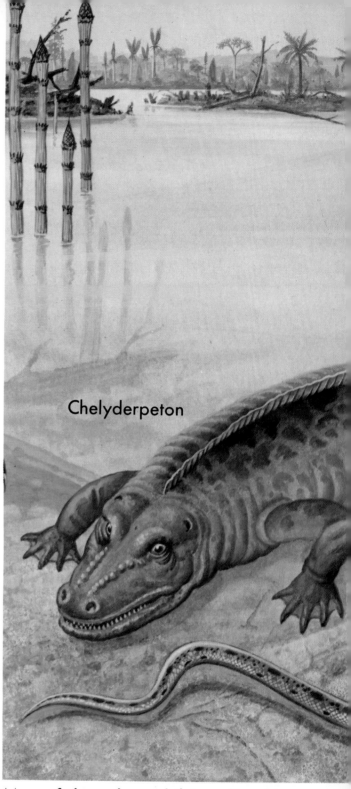

Chelyderpeton

Sometimes we find fossilized tree trunks, like the one in this picture. We call these fossils petrified wood. They often contain bright colours.

Many fish and amphibians lived in the swamps. We sometimes find their bones in coal. All sort of creatures lived in the deep piles of leaves in the forests. The centipede in the picture on the left was 2 metres long.

Dragonfly

Ophiderpeton

The trees dropped their leaves and stems into the water of the swamps. Over millions of years these leaves and stems were pressed tightly together. They dried up and turned into coal.

Under the great trees the ground was covered with thick clumps of ferns. Giant dragonflies flew in the steamy atmosphere. The picture on the left shows the fossil of the leaf of a fern.

Early Texas amphibians

In the Permian Period, about 270 million years ago, many more types of amphibians evolved. The larger ones, like Eryops, lived in the water and ate fish. Archeria had lots of small teeth. It probably ate the smaller animals that lived in the water. The fossils of these amphibians were found in Texas.

Diadectes

Cacops

Some amphibians lived their lives on land. Little Cacops was about 40 centimetres long. It lived on worms and snails. Larger Seymouria probably ate other amphibians. Diadectes had flattened teeth and a bulky body. It was probably the first land animal to eat plants.

Eryops

Seymouria

Diplocaulus

Archeria

This little snake is just hatching out of its egg. The eggs of reptiles have shells. The eggs of amphibians do not have shells.

The tadpole spends its life in the water. It cannot live on land. It breathes through gills. Tadpoles have horny teeth to scrape off food from the plants in the water.

From egg to frog

This is the life cycle of a living amphibian, the frog. The eggs of amphibians only have a covering of jelly. The eggs dry up easily.
So amphibians lay their eggs in water.
The jelly stops the eggs clogging together in the water.

The picture on the left shows a mass of spawn laid in a pond by a frog. Each egg develops into a tadpole. The tadpole wriggles out of the jelly. It uses its long tail to swim, just like a fish.

As it gets bigger, the tadpole gets ready to live on land. Its tail gets shorter. It grows arms and legs. The tadpole's gills get smaller and then disappear. It grows lungs instead, so that it can breathe air.

The adult frog can hop about on land. It can swim in the water too. It feeds on insects and snails. It has a damp skin. The frog breathes both through its skin and through its lungs.

PREHISTORIC REPTILES

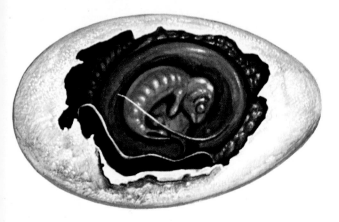

The first reptile is called Hylonomus. It lived about 300 million years ago. It looked like a small lizard.

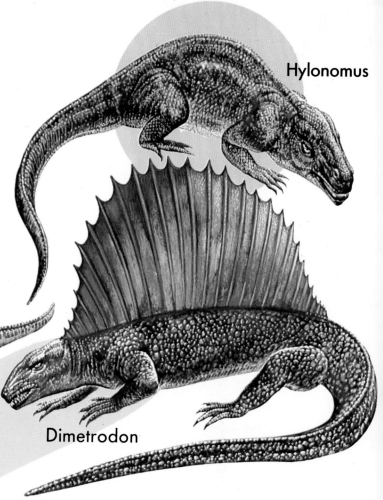

Hylonomus

Reptiles have an egg with a shell. The egg has its own supply of food and water. The shell protects the baby reptile from being eaten. It does not have to begin life in the water. The reptile lays her eggs on land, not in the water.

Dimetrodon

Cynognathus

Erythrotherium

Many different types of reptiles evolved in a short time. Some of them are called mammal-like reptiles. One of them had a strange shape along the top of its back. This may have helped it to get heat from the sun when the animal was cold. These mammal-like reptiles developed into the first mammals.

Reptiles developed in another important way. They developed into great dinosaurs.

Euparkeria

Apatosaurus

Stegosaurus

Iguanodon

Tyrannosaurus

There were two groups of dinosaurs. One group of dinosaurs like Iguanodon and Stegosaurus ate plants. The other group included plant-eaters and meat-eaters.

Triceratops

Early dinosaurs

Dinosaurs were the most powerful creatures on earth for 130 million years. Here are some that lived during the Jurassic Period. Apatosaurus and Brachiosaurus were the biggest plant-eating land animals that we know.

Stegosaurus

Apatosaurus

Brachiosaurus

Scelidosaurus

Megalosaurus

Brachiosaurus and Apatosaurus ate plants. Not all the plant-eating dinosaurs were giants. Stegosaurus and Scelidosaurus were smaller. They had an armour of bone in their skins. This protected them from the big meat-eating dinosaurs like great Megalosaurus.

Later dinosaurs

These dinosaurs lived during the next period of time. It was called the Cretaceous Period. These were the last of the dinosaurs.

Corythosaurus

Anatosaurus

Tyrannosaurus

Styracosaurus

The biggest meat-eating dinosaur we know about lived during this time. It is called Tyrannosaurus and it could run very fast on its back legs. Some of the plant-eating dinosaurs, like Styracosaurus, had horns on their heads. They used the horns to protect themselves from the attacks of meat-eaters.

This picture gives some idea of the size of the large dinosaurs. The head of Tyrannosaurus was about $1\frac{1}{2}$ metres long. Its body measured nearly $14\frac{1}{2}$ metres from head to tail, and it stood over $5\frac{1}{2}$ metres tall.

Dinosaurs and living animals

Dinosaurs were reptiles and laid eggs. They laid the eggs in shallow holes which they dug in the ground. Some nests with 20 eggs have been found. Can you imagine the size of a dinosaur's egg? The biggest egg found was 25 centimetres long. It was as large as 60 chicken's eggs put together.

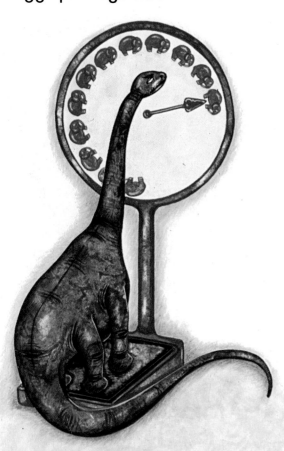

Brachiosaurus was really the dinosaur version of a giraffe. But it was much taller and heavier than a giraffe.

Dinosaurs did not have any hair on their skin. So they quickly became cold when the weather was cool.

The biggest dinosaur of all was Brachiosaurus. It weighed as much as 12 elephants. It had long front legs and a very long neck, so that it could eat the leaves of trees.

It is difficult to imagine the strange world of creatures that have now all died out. Many people think that the dinosaurs were all gigantic. But some of them were quite small.
Little Compsognathus was only the size of a chicken.

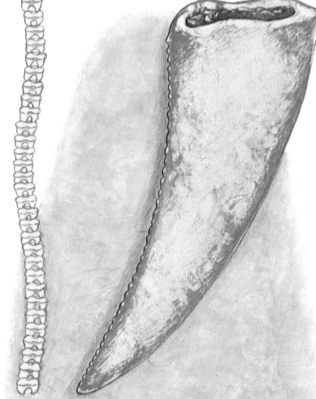

Animals that eat meat have sharp cutting teeth. The teeth of the great Tyrannosaurus were as long as 30 human teeth. Other dinosaurs had hundreds of teeth in the back of their jaws. They used them to grind up the plants they ate.

Sea monsters

While the dinosaurs lived on land, other strange reptiles lived in the seas. Tylosaurus was a relative of the lizard, and ate fish. The largest of the sea reptiles was Kronosaurus. It had a large head. It caught and ate other sea reptiles living in the sea.

Tylosaurus

Plesiosaurs had strong limbs like paddles. They used these to push themselves through the water. Some of them had long rubbery necks. Some Plesiosaurs ate fish.

Kronosaurus

Ichthyosaurs swam like fish. They lashed their tails from side to side. They had a fin on their backs. Their long snout hid many teeth. They used it to catch and eat fish. These reptiles only had small limbs.

Birds and flying reptiles

These strange creatures were flying reptiles. They are called pterosaurs. They had leathery wings like those of a bat. Each wing stretched between the body and the long fourth finger of the hand. Pterosaurs folded up their wings when they walked on the ground. They were covered with hair to keep themselves warm.

Pteranodon was one of the biggest of the pterosaurs. It had no teeth. It used its long horny beak to catch fish in the sea.

Rhamphorhynchus was only the size of a sparrow. It had sharp teeth and ate insects. Its long tail ended in a little rudder. It used this to steer itself through the air.

Archaeopteryx was the first bird. Its body was covered with feathers. But it had a long bony tail like a reptile. Archaeopteryx also still had teeth in its beak. The fingers on its wings had little claws.

Early birds

Birds have a covering of feathers. So they are always warm. Like reptiles, they lay eggs. The eggs are laid in a nest and the parent birds keep them warm. Most birds can fly. This means that they can make their nests in high places like trees.

But some birds like the penguin and the ostrich are no longer able to fly.

Birds could escape from enemies on the ground by flying away. Sometimes they landed in places where there were no fierce enemies.

Phororhachos lived in South America. It had a head as big as a horse's head, and strong feet with claws.

Hesperornis was a bird that lived at the same time as the dinosaurs. It could not fly. Instead, it used its strong hind limbs to swim in the sea. It used its sharp teeth to catch fish.

44

Birds no longer needed to fly to stay alive. So those that could not fly could survive. Over millions of years the birds gradually changed.

Their legs grew longer to run about. Their wings grew smaller. The birds got bigger and fiercer. Sometimes they ate other animals.

The moa was over 3 metres tall. It lived on plant food. People hunted this animal until it died out.

When the dinosaurs died out, there were no large mammals that ate other animals. But some big meat-eating birds developed. Diatryma was one of these. It was taller than a man.

The end of the dinosaurs

All the dinosaurs died out at about the same time. We still do not know why this happened. Some people think new types of plants evolved. The new plants might have contained juices that poisoned the dinosaurs. But we know some of the dinosaurs evolved after these plants. So they must have been used to eating them.

Other people think that the world became hotter and hotter. The big dinosaurs would not have been able to find shady places to keep cool. But the small dinosaurs died out too.

Perhaps the dinosaurs all died out because the world got too cold. But then they would have been able to survive in the hotter parts. Before the dinosaurs died out, the temperature was the same all through the year. Then it changed. The summer became hotter and the winter colder. Perhaps the dinosaurs could not live with these changes.

The dinosaurs were reptiles, and laid eggs. Did the little mammals eat their eggs? Was that why the dinosaurs died out? But the mammals and dinosaurs had lived together for millions of years. So we still cannot be sure why the dinosaurs all died.

THE FIRST MAMMALS

After the dinosaurs died out, the little mammals spread throughout the world. Mammals are different from reptiles. They usually do not lay eggs. Instead, the young mammal grows for a long time inside its mother's body. After it is born, it feeds on its mother's milk. Mammals are covered with hair to keep warm.

Mammals are more clever than reptiles or birds. They can learn many things. Young mammals stay with their parents. The parents teach them how to find food and how to keep away from danger. Some families of mammals stay in groups. They protect themselves from enemies.

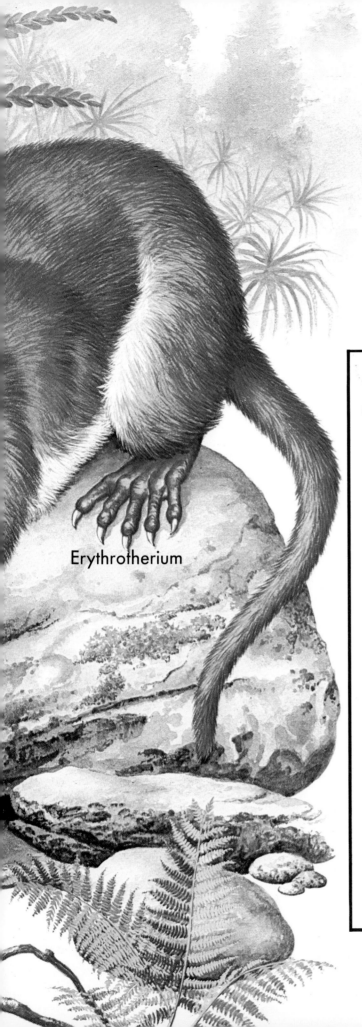

The first mammals evolved when the dinosaurs were still alive. They were only small. They fed on insects, snails and lizards. Little Erythrotherium was one of the first mammals. Many new types of mammals developed after the dinosaurs died out. They grew much bigger. Some fed on meat, others ate only plants.

Erythrotherium

Bats are mammals that can fly. Their hands have changed into wings.

Dolphins, whales and seals are mammals that live in the sea.

The platypus is one of the very few living mammals that still lays eggs.

The first elephants

Elephants have evolved an easy way to reach the leaves on tall trees. Their upper lip has grown into a long flexible trunk. They can use the trunk to pull down branches from trees. Elephants are also strong enough to push down small trees. They do this so that they can eat the leaves more comfortably.

Moeritherium was the first elephant. It was only the size of a pig. It had a very short trunk.

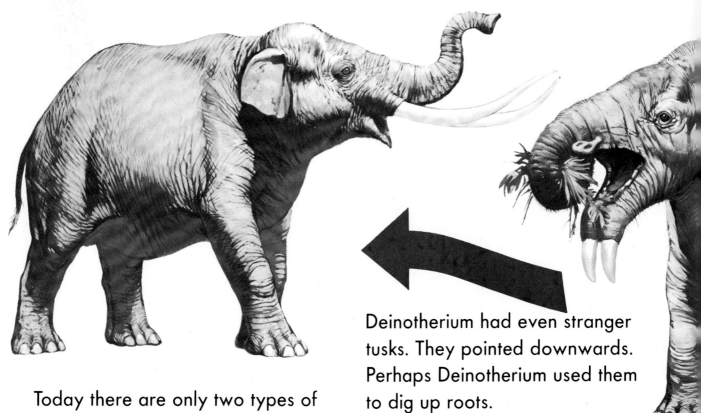

Deinotherium had even stranger tusks. They pointed downwards. Perhaps Deinotherium used them to dig up roots.

Today there are only two types of elephant, the Indian elephant and the African. The Indian elephant you can see here has a domed head. It has ears which are much smaller than the African elephant's ears.

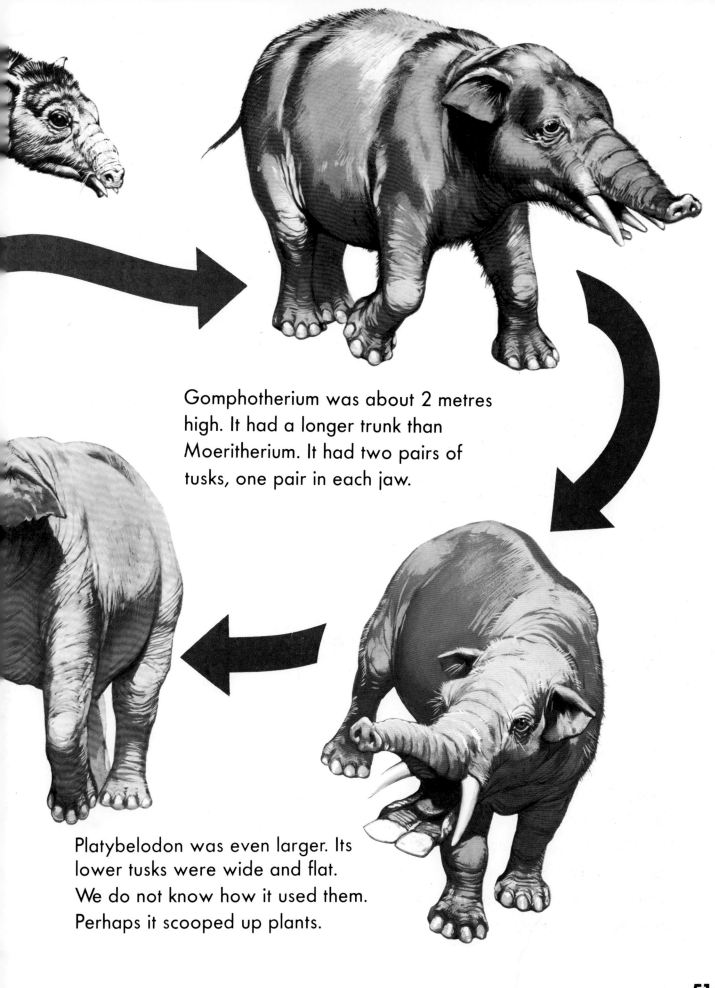

Gomphotherium was about 2 metres
high. It had a longer trunk than
Moeritherium. It had two pairs of
tusks, one pair in each jaw.

Platybelodon was even larger. Its
lower tusks were wide and flat.
We do not know how it used them.
Perhaps it scooped up plants.

Strange mammals

Many strange types of mammal lived in the past. Some had horns to defend themselves. Some mammals were bigger than any land animal alive today. Synthetoceras had a long horn on its nose. The horn ended in two sharp points. It had horns in front of its ears, too.

Indricotherium is the biggest land mammal that ever lived. Its shoulders were nearly 6 metres above the ground. Its head was 1½ metres long. It ate the leaves of trees.

 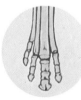

The first horse was only the size of a dog. It is called Hyracotherium. It lived in forests and fed on the leaves of trees and bushes.

Horses gradually became bigger and bigger. They moved out onto the grasslands to eat grass. The ground there was harder than in the forests.

Uintatherium ate plants. It was
4 metres long. There were strange
bony lumps on its head and jaws.
These may have protected it from
the attacks of meat-eating animals.

Smilodon was a very fierce meat
eater. It had long sharp fangs. It used
these to bite through the thick skins
of the animals it hunted. It only
hunted the animals that ate plants.

On the hard ground, horses did not
need such big feet as they did on the
soft earth of the forests. Their feet
became smaller and lighter.

Today horses only have a single toe
and a hoof on each foot. They have
big strong teeth so that they can eat
the hard grass.

THE EVOLUTION OF MAN

Today scientists know a great deal about the development of early man. Long, long ago, our ancestors spent a lot of their time in the trees. But they could also walk on the ground.

Proconsul

Ramapithecus

Australopithecus

Leakey's man

Over millions of years, man began to spend more time on the ground.

His body became straighter, and gradually he was able to run faster.

This picture is of a great valley in Africa called the Olduvai Gorge. Many fossils of early man have been found here. The ancestors of man had to leave their life in the trees because the climate was changing. The weather was becoming colder and the forests were becoming smaller. Instead, there were scattered trees and grassland. Our ancestors lived and found food there.

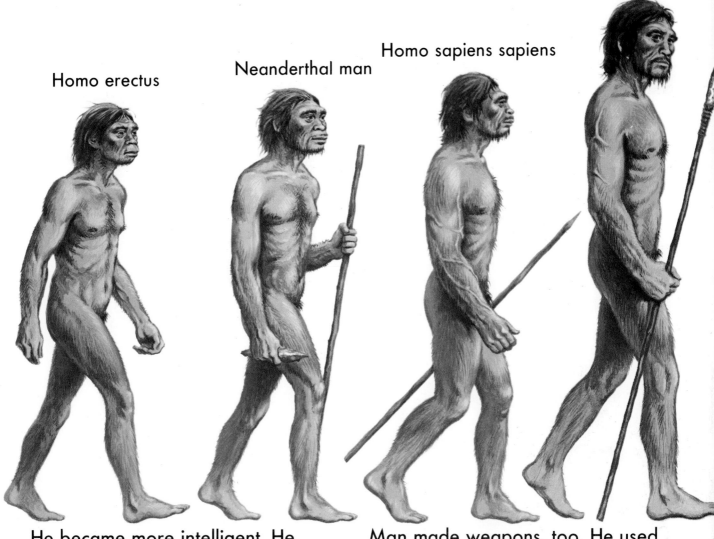

Homo erectus

Neanderthal man

Homo sapiens sapiens

Cro Magnon man

He became more intelligent. He made tools out of stone and wood.

Man made weapons, too. He used them to hunt animals.

Man had learned to draw and paint long before he lived in towns. He carved designs on his bone tools. His beautiful paintings can be seen on the walls of ancient caves. The paintings and the carvings show the animals that early man was hunting. The artist may have drawn them to bring luck in the next day's hunting. They may also have been part of his magic and religion.

Australopithecus

Australopithecus was about 120 centimetres tall and walked almost upright. His brain was quite small and he had a face like an ape.

Australopithecus probably ate anything he could find. He collected fruit and berries, chased lizards and mice, and chewed on bones.

He hunted in groups to catch bigger animals. Australopithecus probably used animal bones as weapons. He made simple stone tools. He sheltered in caves during bad weather.

Leakey's man

Early man was not a common creature so the bones of fossil men are not often found. But we know that man continued to evolve. Dr Leakey recently discovered a type of fossil man which nobody knew about before. Now that man has learnt to grow his own food crops, he is one of the commonest animals.

1

This shows how we reconstruct the newly discovered fossils of early men. First, the scientist joins the fragments of the skull together.

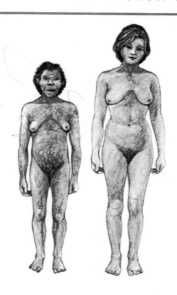

As mankind evolved, the size of adult people increased. They grew bigger because they found more things to eat. Bigger people could run faster to escape from their enemies.

Dr Leakey's man lived in places where there were many lakes. He may have lived on fish as well as other animals. He built low shelters of stones to keep out the wind.

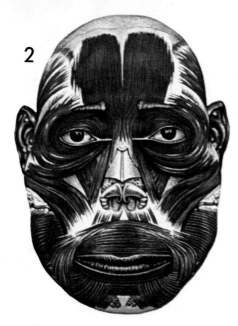

2

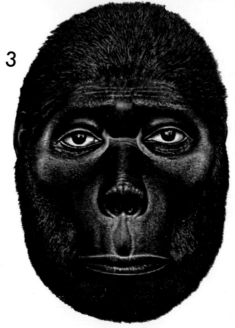

3

Then the scientist reconstructs the muscles of the face. These muscles moved the eyebrows, lips and jaws. The ears and nose are added, too.

Finally the scientist covers the face with skin and hair. Of course, we do not know the colour of the skin, or how much hair there was.

Homo erectus

The type of man who lived before modern man is called Homo erectus. He lived about 1½ million years ago. He was bigger and more intelligent than Australopithecus. Homo erectus learnt to use fire. He used it to cook his food. The fire protected him from wild animals, and kept him warm.

Once people began to live in large groups, they must have learned to use words. These were probably only noises at first, to warn of danger or to call each other. Gradually they learned to use a special noise or word for each animal they hunted. This is how language began.

Neanderthal man

After Homo erectus the next type of man was called Neanderthal man. He had heavy ridges over his eyes, and a sloping chin and forehead. But his brain was as big as ours. He made many different types of stone tools. Neanderthal man hunted animals like the aurochs. Their skins kept him warm during the winter.

Some stone tools were used for skinning animals. Others were used for cutting up the animals, or for cleaning the skins to make clothes.

Neanderthal man seems to have had a religion. He carefully buried his dead. Sometimes he placed flowers and ornaments in the grave. He also put stone tools and weapons with the body for use in the next life.

DID YOU KNOW?

Some people think there is a monster living in a lake in Scotland. They call it the Loch Ness monster. If it is there it is probably a Plesiosaur. It is a living fossil.

In 1853 a giant model was made of an Iguanodon. It was made for the Crystal Palace Exhibition. A dinner was given inside the Iguanodon for 21 people.

Tanystropheus lived in the sea. It used its long neck to catch fish. But when Tany was only young it lived on the land. Some scientists think it may have caught insects.

Pachycephalosaurs had very thick skulls. They were just like helmets. Sometimes the male animals had fights. Then they banged their heads together to see who was stronger.

Cold-Blooded Animals

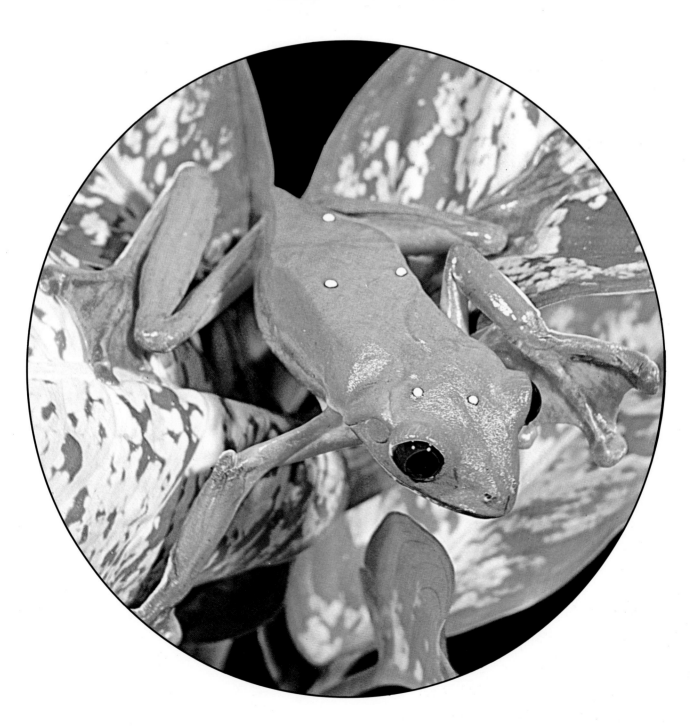

COLD-BLOODED ANIMALS

All animals are related to each other. They are divided into two groups. You can see the cold-blooded animals in the blue circles. Their bodies are at about the same temperature as their surroundings. The warm-blooded animals are in the pink circles. Their bodies have a high temperature which always stays the same.

frog

crocodile

fish

starfish

shark

tortoise

sea-urchin

worm

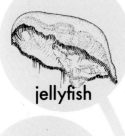

jellyfish

sea anemone

coral

snail

octopus

sponge

mussel

66

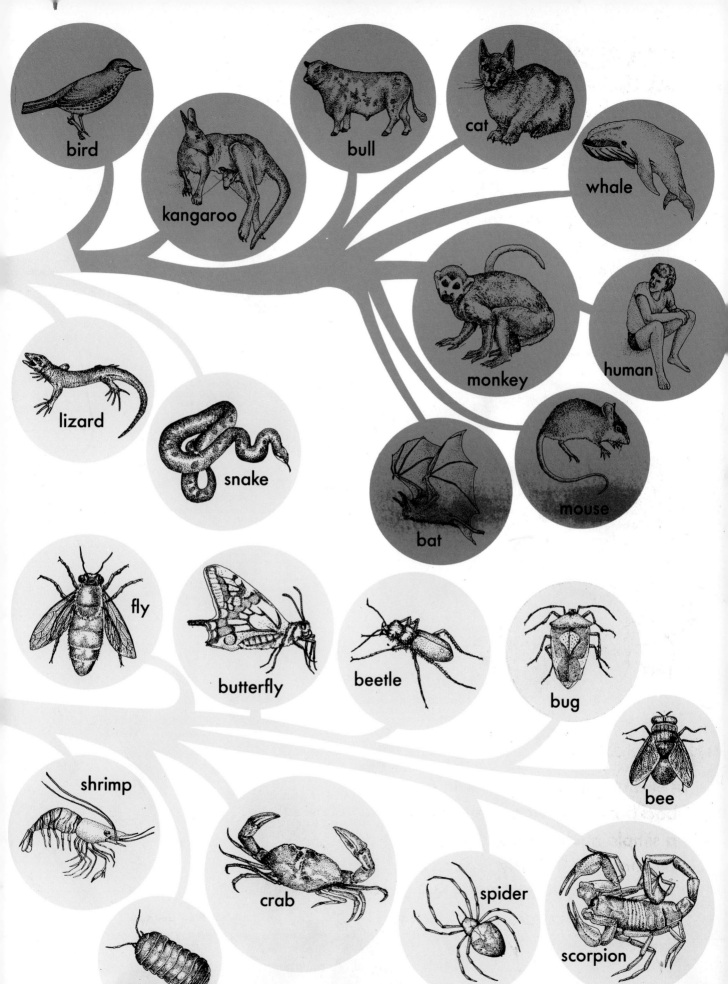

bird

kangaroo

bull

cat

whale

monkey

human

lizard

snake

bat

mouse

fly

butterfly

beetle

bug

bee

shrimp

crab

spider

scorpion

woodlice

SIMPLE ANIMALS

Mammals, birds, reptiles, amphibians and fishes have skeletons of bone. Their skeletons have a backbone with rows of bones called vertebrae. These animals are called vertebrates. You can feel your vertebrae in the middle of your back. Animals that do not have backbones are called invertebrates.

The boy has a skeleton with a backbone. The worm he is holding is a simple animal. It does not have a skeleton and its body is floppy. The crab's body and legs are covered with a hard shell which is a kind of skeleton.

sea anemone

The sea anemone has a soft body. Its tentacles sting fish and push food into its mouth. When the tide goes out the anemone closes up its tentacles. This keeps it moist.

sponge

Sponges are animals, not plants. The bath sponge that we use is the skeleton of the animal. It is made up of strong fibres. Sponges live mainly in warm, shallow seas.

Animals of the garden

The garden is the home of many simple animals without backbones. You can find these animals on plants, in the earth or in ponds. Sometimes you have to look very carefully. Slugs and snails have soft bodies. They do not like hot, dry weather. When it is hot, snails hide in their shells. Slugs creep into the shade.

ladybird

wolf spider

greenflies

ants

beetle

slugs

earthworm

snail

earwig

Earthworms live underground but they come up to eat leaves at night. Moths also come out at night. You can see most of the animals in this picture in the daytime. Butterflies and bees fly from flower to flower. Ladybirds and spiders eat other animals. Ants eat a substance called honeydew which is made by greenflies.

white admiral

bumble bee

honey bees

large heath butterfly

peacock butterfly

garden snail

wasps

Animals of the rock pool

The seashore is a very good place to look for animals. When the tide goes out, sea creatures are left in rock pools. Can you see the prawns and blennies swimming in this pool? Sea anemones, mussels and barnacles are fixed to the rocks, but limpets and topshells can crawl around slowly.

The giant clam lives on coral reefs. It grows up to one metre across and weighs up to 250 kilograms.

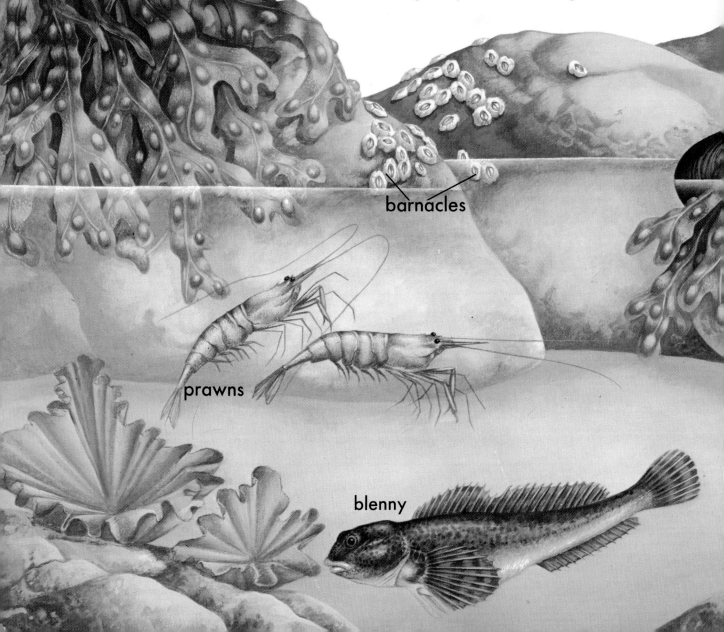

barnacles

prawns

blenny

Starfish live in the sea, but they sometimes come into rock pools. They eat mussels and other shellfish.

limpets

barnacles

mussels

sea anemones

blenny

topshells

Octopuses and squids

'Molluscs' is the name given to animals such as snails, winkles, clams and squids. All molluscs have soft bodies. Some of them are protected by hard shells and they move slowly. Octopuses and squids are molluscs but they don't have a shell. They live in the sea and can move very fast.

octopus

An octopus has eight arms. It walks on the sea bed or swims by squirting a jet of water. It kills its prey with a poisonous bite.

A squid has ten arms. It also moves by squirting out a jet of water which pushes it forwards. Giant squids grow up to 20 metres in length. This giant squid is having a long battle with a sperm whale.

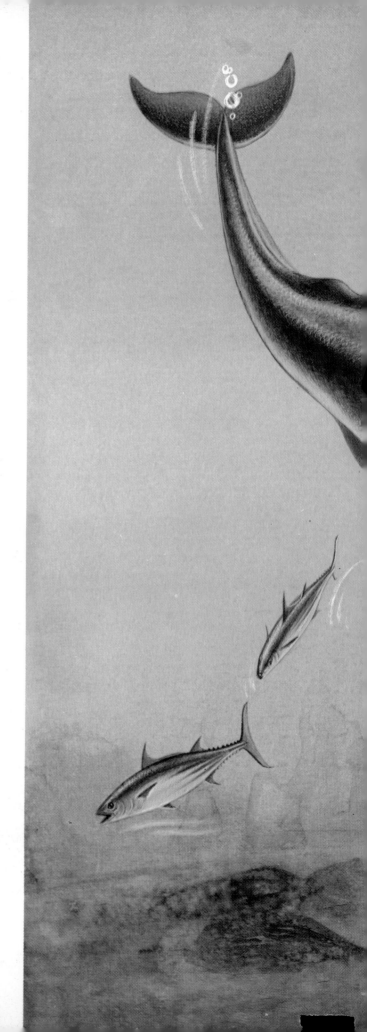

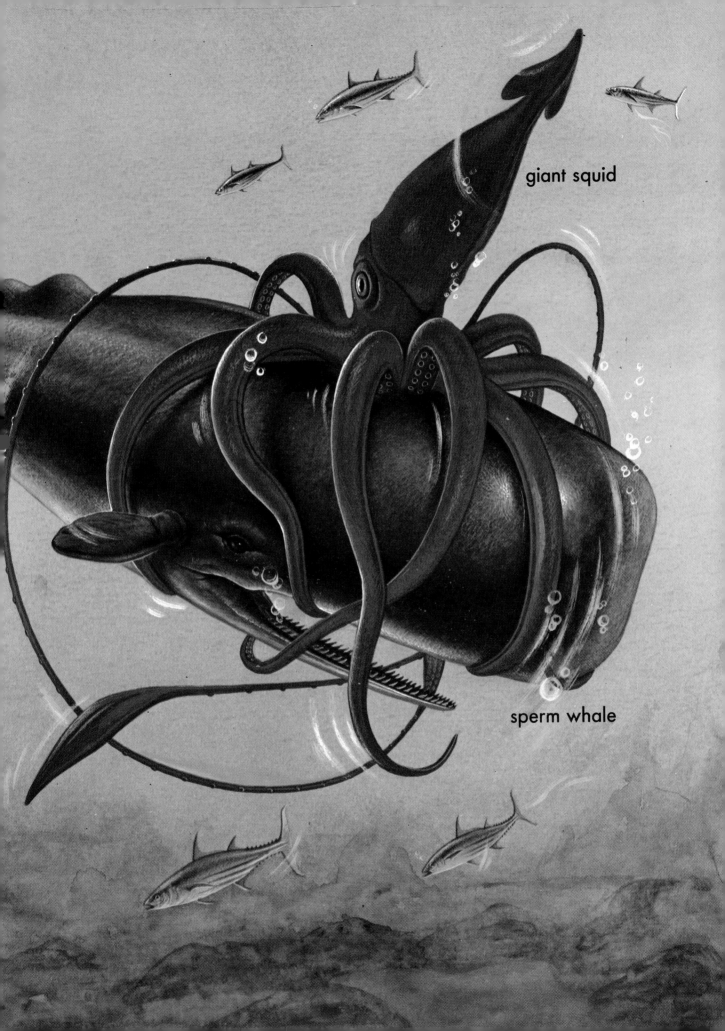

giant squid

sperm whale

ANIMALS WITH MANY LEGS

Most animals with backbones have four legs or fins. Some stand upright on their back legs. Others use their tail as a kind of third leg. Animals without backbones have all sorts of arrangements of legs. Some of them have very strange ways of walking. Some animals, like the worm, have no legs at all.

0 legs

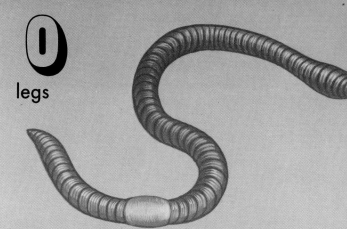

A worm has no legs. It moves by pushing out its head and then pulling the rest of its body forwards.

1 leg

A snail crawls on its stomach which is a kind of foot. It lays a sticky trail to help it slide along.

2 legs

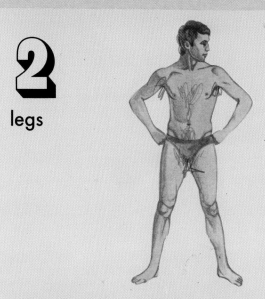

A man stands upright on his two legs.

3 two legs and a tail

Kangaroos use their tail for balance.

4 legs

Bears usually walk on all fours.

5

four
legs
and a tail

This monkey uses its tail as a fifth leg to help when it is climbing through the trees.

6

legs

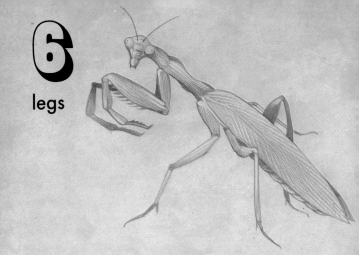

The six-legged mantis is an insect. It catches food with its front legs.

8

legs

Spiders have eight legs. The extra pair of legs makes them different from insects.

10

legs

Crabs have ten legs. The front pair are claws which are used for fighting.

30+

legs

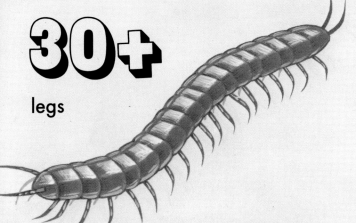

A centipede has one pair of legs under each section of its body.

60+

legs

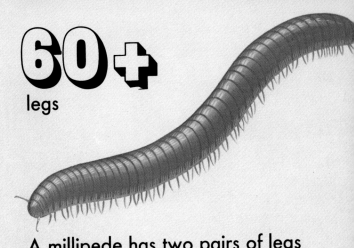

A millipede has two pairs of legs under each section of its body.

Crabs and lobsters

Crabs and lobsters are called crustaceans. Their bodies are covered with an outside skeleton. This is their shell. When they are growing, they shed their shell and grow a new one. They have five pairs of legs. The front pair are large claws which they use for fighting and for catching food. Most crabs and lobsters live in the sea.

The shore crab is very common in rock pools and on the beach. It eats any animals that it can seize with its claws. It also uses its claws to defend itself. If you try to pick up a shore crab, it may nip you with its claws.

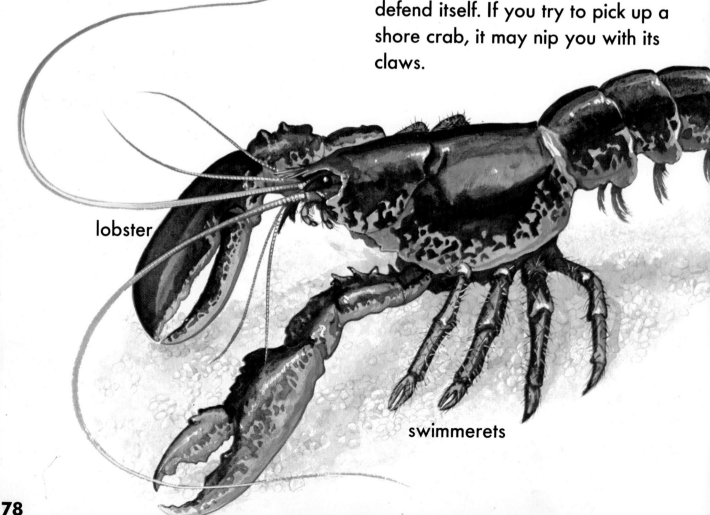

lobster

swimmerets

Fiddler crabs have one huge claw. They use it for signalling to other crabs. Fiddler crabs are found round the coast of Britain.

Lobsters have very long bodies and several pairs of legs which they use for swimming. These legs are called swimmerets. Fishermen catch lobsters in lobster pots like the one on the right. The lobster climbs into the pot to get food but cannot get out again.

Shrimps and barnacles

Shrimps and barnacles are both crustaceans but they look very different. A shrimp looks like a tiny lobster and can swim very well. A barnacle looks like a limpet. It has a hard shell. When a barnacle is covered with water its shell opens. Pieces of food are washed into its mouth when it waves its legs around.

Baby barnacles float in the sea. When they are older they fix themselves to something solid. They usually fix themselves to rocks. Sometimes they stick to the sides and bottoms of ships. In the picture above you can see men scraping barnacles off the side of a ship.

This shrimp is living in a razor-shell, where it is safe from its enemies. It only comes out to feed.

When the tide goes out, barnacles shut their shells and are safe until the tide comes in again. Shrimps and other creatures are often trapped in rock pools. Always put back animals you find in pools.

Spiders and scorpions

All insects have six legs. Spiders and scorpions have eight legs so they are not insects. Scorpions have a front pair of claws like a lobster. They have long bodies and their tail has a sting in the tip. Spiders have round bodies.

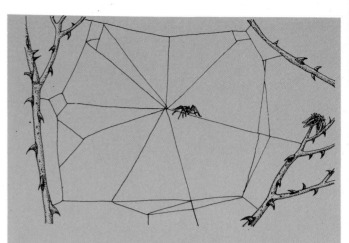

To build a web the spider first makes a frame of silk threads.

scorpion

Scorpions use their claws for catching food. They only use their sting to defend themselves.

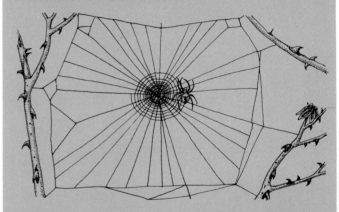

Next the spider lays a spiral of silk thread on the frame.

This spider has caught a fly in its web, and has wrapped it in silk before eating it.

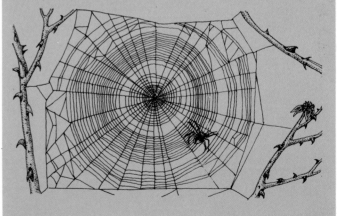

When the spider has finished making the web, it sits and waits for flies to be trapped in it.

This spider is waiting patiently in its web. When a fly is caught by the sticky silk it struggles. This struggling warns the spider. The spider runs across the web and kills the fly by poisoning it.

INSECTS

You can recognize an insect because it has three pairs of legs and its body has three parts. Most insects lay eggs but some give birth to baby insects. Some young insects look like their parents. They are called nymphs. Others have soft, worm-like bodies. These are called caterpillars or grubs. They change into adults inside a case. This case is called a pupa.

The life of a butterfly or moth starts with an egg. You can often find insect eggs on leaves.

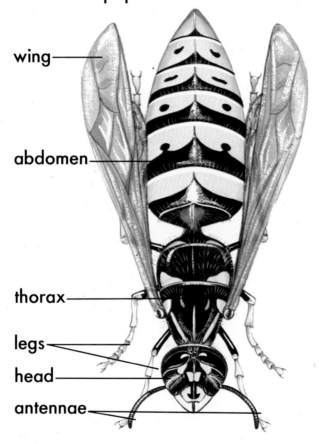

wing

abdomen

thorax

legs

head

antennae

The body of an insect, like this wasp, has a head, a thorax and an abdomen. The wings and legs are joined to the thorax.

The pupa splits open and the adult butterfly or moth crawls out. Adults do not usually live very long.

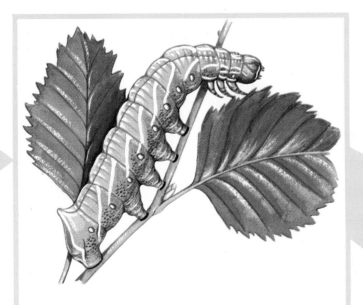

The egg hatches into a caterpillar.
The caterpillar spends most of its
time eating. It grows very fast.

chrysalis

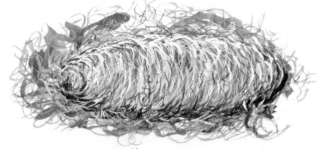

silk cocoon

The caterpillar turns into a pupa.
A butterfly pupa is called a chrysalis.
Moths spin a silk cocoon.

Butterflies and moths

The wings of butterflies and moths are covered with tiny scales. They are often very brightly coloured. The best way to tell a butterfly from a moth is to look at its antennae. A butterfly's antennae end in knobs. A moth usually has feathery antennae. Most butterflies feed on nectar, from flowers.

garden tiger moth

Most moths fly at night and hide by day. The garden tiger moth cannot hide very well. It is too brightly coloured. These colours warn birds that the moth has a nasty taste, and so they leave it well alone.

elephant hawk moth

The bull's eye moth in the picture above and the emperor moth have 'eyes' on their wings. These 'eyes' scare away birds that may try to eat the moths. Most moths have wings that fasten together with a tiny hook. Butterflies do not have these hooks.

emperor moth

monarch
butterfly

swallowtail
butterfly

common blue
butterfly

peacock
butterfly

Butterflies do not look as if they are strong fliers but some kinds travel long distances. The monarch butterfly of America flies 3000 kilometres to spend the winter in warm countries. Sometimes it flies across the Atlantic Ocean. Swallowtails and blue butterflies usually stay in one place.

Brazilian skipper butterfly

Many adult insects die in the autumn. Peacock butterflies, like the one on the left, are different. They live in hollow trees and in buildings during the winter. In the spring they wake up and fly away. You can see them in many different places. They live in parks, gardens and forests.

Flies

Most insects have two pairs of wings. Flies have only one pair. Instead of the rear pair of wings they have two tiny stalks. These stalks help the fly to keep its balance when it is flying. Some flies are very dangerous because they carry disease. Some mosquitoes carry a disease called malaria.

You must never let house-flies walk on food in the kitchen or in the shops. These pictures tell you why.

Flies carry germs on their feet. Germs cause disease. When you eat the food, you also eat the germs.

Daddy-long-legs is another name for the crane-fly. It has long, thin legs which break off easily. The grubs of crane-flies are called leather-jackets. They live underground.

The germs soon make you ill. So always cover food. It is best to keep food in a refrigerator.

Hover-flies look like wasps but they cannot sting you. They can hover and fly backwards just like a helicopter.

House-flies have feet which have two claws and a rough pad. These help the fly to walk on walls and ceilings.

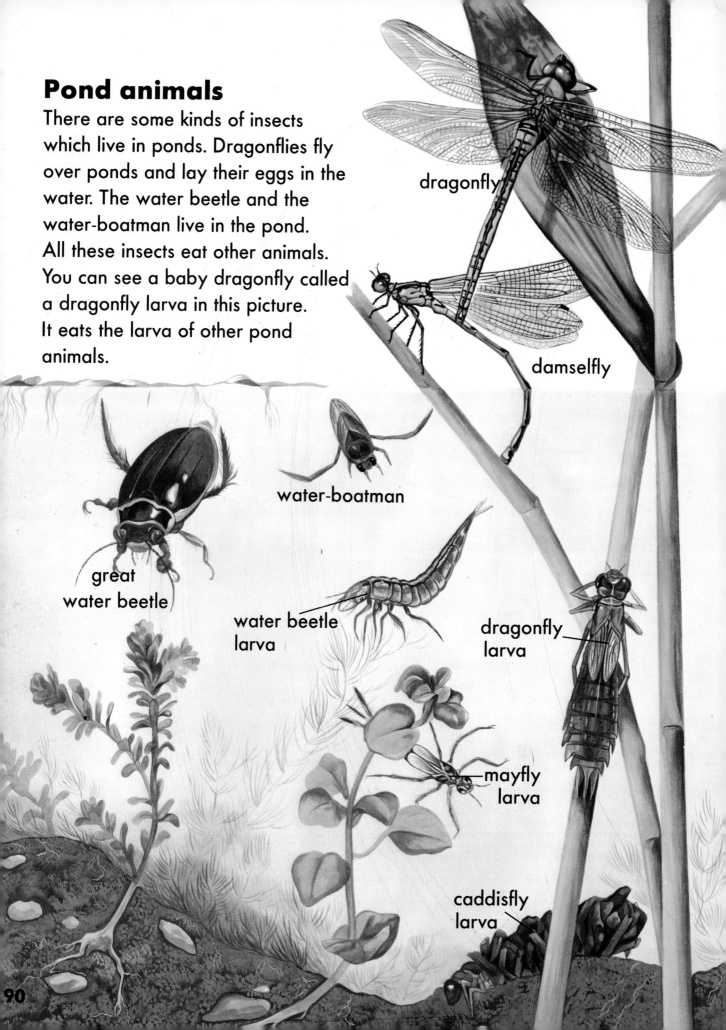

Pond animals

There are some kinds of insects which live in ponds. Dragonflies fly over ponds and lay their eggs in the water. The water beetle and the water-boatman live in the pond. All these insects eat other animals. You can see a baby dragonfly called a dragonfly larva in this picture. It eats the larva of other pond animals.

dragonfly

damselfly

water-boatman

great water beetle

water beetle larva

dragonfly larva

mayfly larva

caddisfly larva

Termites

Termites live in huge nests, like the one on the right. These nests are like castles made of hard earth. Often the nests are as much as five metres in height. Termites live in warm countries like Australia and parts of North and South America. Their main food is wood. They often attack wooden buildings.

A termite nest is the home of a queen termite and thousands of worker termites. There is also a king termite. The enormous queen termite grows up to five centimetres long. All she does is eat and lay eggs.

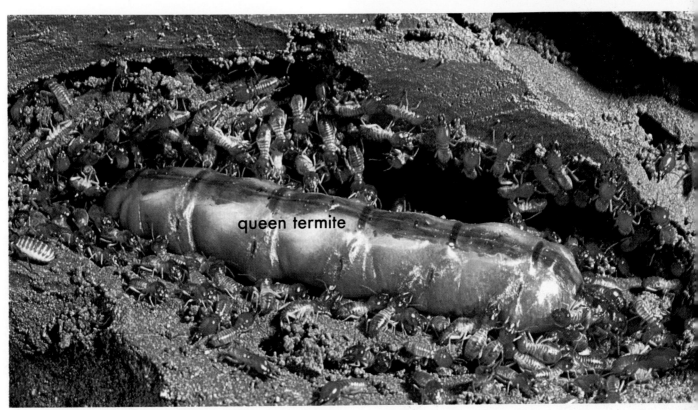

queen termite

Grasshoppers, crickets and locusts

Grasshoppers and crickets have long back legs. They can jump well. If you try to catch one it will leap away. They also have wings for flying. Grasshoppers and crickets usually come out in warm weather. You can see grasshoppers in the daytime but crickets mostly come out at night. Locusts are a kind of grasshopper.

The skins of insects cannot stretch. As insects grow they shed their old skins and grow new ones which are larger. This grasshopper is climbing out of its old skin.

Locusts live in hot countries. Sometimes they gather in great swarms. These swarms are called 'plagues of locusts'. Young locusts are called hoppers. They cannot fly. Swarms of winged adults and hoppers can destroy fields of crops.

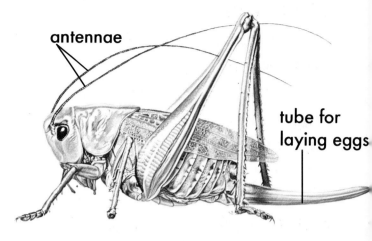

antennae

tube for laying eggs

Crickets have longer antennae than grasshoppers. This female cricket has a long tube at the end of her body. She pushes this tube into the ground and lays her eggs through it.

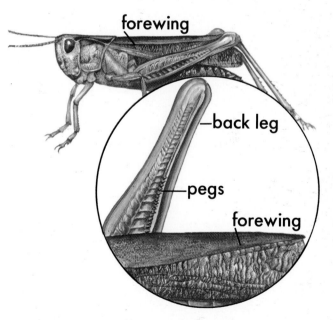

forewing

back leg

pegs

forewing

A grasshopper's back leg has a row of pegs along one side. It 'sings' by rubbing its back leg against its forewing. The picture in the circle above is a close-up of the grasshopper's leg and forewing.

Beetles and bugs

Beetles have hard front wing cases which are often brightly coloured. These protect the delicate back wings. A bug is an insect. Its mouth has a hollow tube rather like the syringe a doctor uses for injections. The tube has a sharp tip and is used for sucking up food.

greenflies

stag beetles

Greenflies are bugs which suck the sap from plants. Gardeners get rid of greenflies and other bugs because of the damage they cause.

These beetles are called stag beetles because their large jaws look like the antlers of a stag, or male deer. You can see these male stag beetles using their jaws for fighting.

This ladybird is taking off from a plant. You can see its brightly coloured front wings.

Ladybirds are beetles. They eat greenflies and other bugs.

The backswimmer or water-boatman always swims on its back. It rows along with its back legs. It is a bug which sucks the blood of other animals. If you touch a backswimmer it may sting your finger.

Bees wasps and ants

Bees, wasps and ants live in large nests. In each nest there is a female, called a queen, who lays eggs. The eggs hatch into grubs. The queen is helped by the worker insects who look after the nest and collect food. In summer, young queens mate with males and fly away to start new nests.

The young queen bee is accompanied by a crowd of worker bees, called a swarm.

A worker wasp eats ripe fruit. It also catches insects for the young grubs.

swarm

drone

worker

queen

The honey bees which you see flying from flower to flower are workers. They collect nectar and pollen from the flower to make into honey. They have a sting which they use for defending the nest. The queens and male bees, called drones, only leave the nest when they mate.

Worker ants do not have wings like bees and wasps. They have to walk when they are searching for food. They are very small, but they are strong. They can easily carry food many metres back to the nest. The parasol ant on the left is carrying a flower to its nest. Parasol ants eat a fungus that grows on the flower.

FISH

Fish are the oldest animals with backbones that we can find today. Nearly all fish live in water. Lungfish and some other fish can come out on land for a short time. Fish swim by wriggling their tails. Their fins help them to keep their balance and steer. Their bodies are covered with scales.

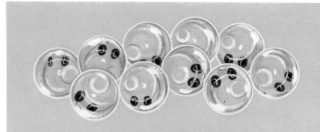

Most fish lay eggs. A few give birth to baby fish. Some fish look after their eggs until they hatch.

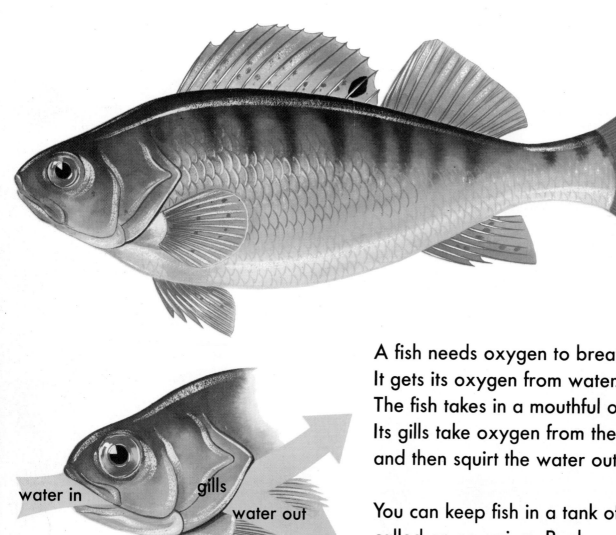

water in   gills   water out

A fish needs oxygen to breathe. It gets its oxygen from water. The fish takes in a mouthful of water. Its gills take oxygen from the water and then squirt the water out again.

You can keep fish in a tank of water called an aquarium. Rocks and weeds make the aquarium look like a pond.

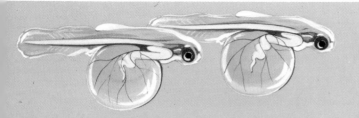

The egg hatches into a larva. At first the larva carries a bag of yolk which it feeds on.

The yolk slowly disappears as the fish grows up. The fully grown fish in this picture has fins and a tail.

fish in aquarium

Sharks

Sharks are fish whose skeletons are made of soft cartilage instead of bone. Most sharks have very sharp teeth and eat fish. Great white sharks are fierce hunters. They sometimes eat men. Blue sharks and leopard sharks can also attack people.

blue shark

thresher shark

great white shark

leopard shark

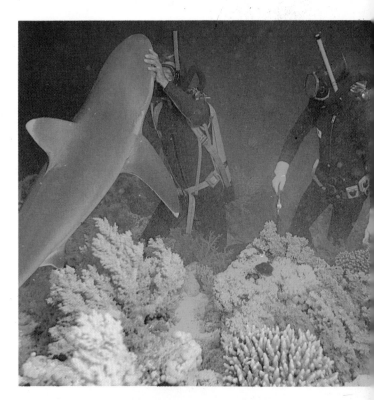

Sharks may be a danger to divers, who often carry weapons to defend themselves. Sharks do not usually attack, as the picture shows.

hammer-head shark

Some sharks give birth to live young. Others lay eggs in cases. These cases are called 'mermaids' purses'.

Sea fish

The coral reefs of tropical seas are
the homes of many amazing fish.
There are strange seahorses and
brightly coloured clownfish and
butterfly fish. Some of the fish that
live in coral reefs are dangerous.
The lionfish has a nasty sting.
The moray eel lives in crevices.
It has sharp teeth and sometimes
bites divers.

seahorse

scorpion fish

clownfish

puffer fish

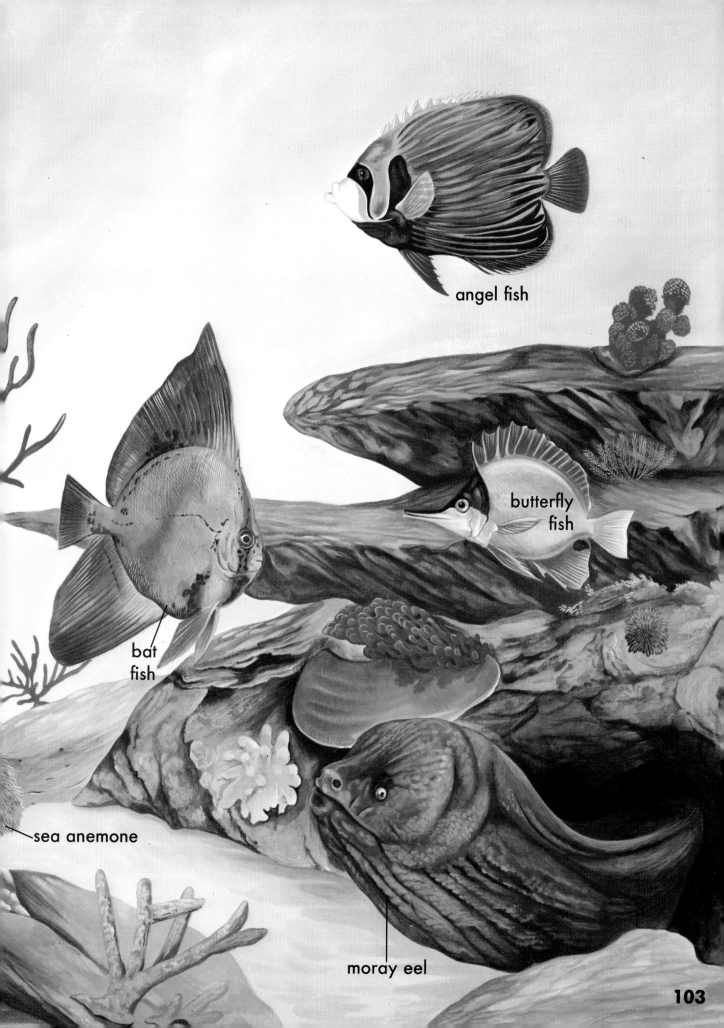

angel fish

butterfly fish

bat fish

sea anemone

moray eel

River fish

These are fish which live in lakes and rivers. Some of them are good to eat. The brown trout lives in clear streams. It eats insects which land on the surface of the water. When it has grown up, the eel swims down the river to the sea. The pike is a fierce hunter which eats other fish. Small fish are eaten by kingfishers as well.

kingfisher

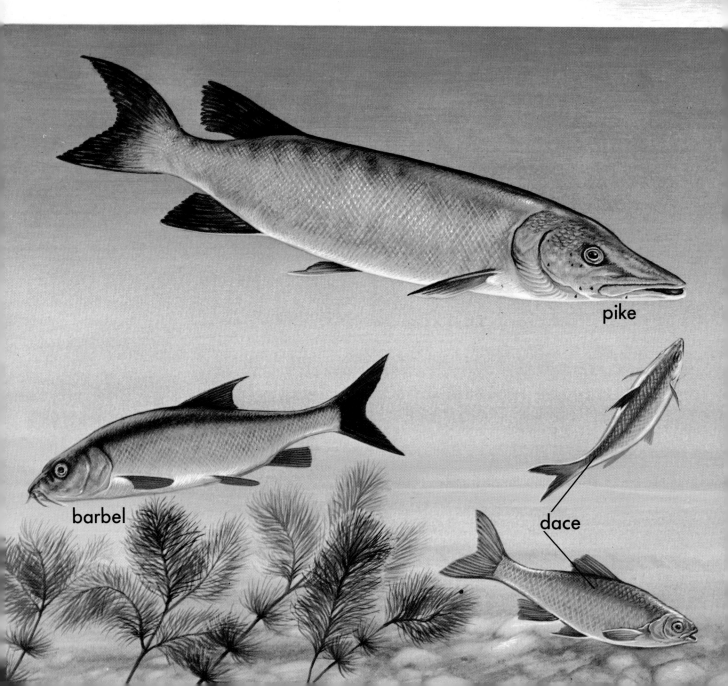

pike

barbel

dace

brown trout

dace

chub

eel

tench

Unusual fish

There are thousands of different kinds of fish. Many of them look very strange. Some have very odd habits. There are fish which live on the bottom of the oceans and have rows of glowing spots on their bodies. There are fish that can glide through the air. There are even fish that can climb trees.

Surgeon fish, like this one on the right, live among coral reefs. They have bones near their tails that are as sharp as a surgeon's knife.

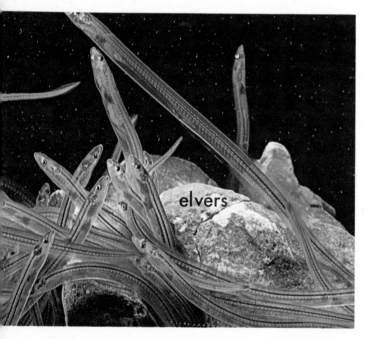

elvers

Baby eels are called elvers. Elvers swim thousands of kilometres from the warm sea where they hatch to the rivers of North America and Europe.

seahorse

The seahorse is one of the oddest fish. It swims by moving the fin on its back. The female lays her eggs in a pouch on the male's belly.
The babies swim out after hatching.

On the left is a puffer fish. This fish can blow up its body like a balloon. This makes it difficult for enemies to swallow.

Amphibians

Amphibians are animals which can live either on land or in the water. Their eggs do not have shells and have to be laid in water. The adults' skin is not fully waterproof and it has to keep moist. A few amphibians do, however, live in dry places.

tiny tadpoles

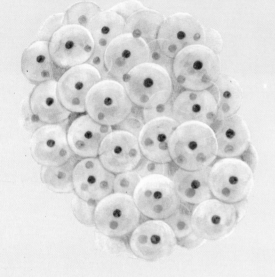

You can see the eggs developing into tiny tadpoles. It takes about two weeks from laying to hatching.

At first, the tadpole has no legs. It looks rather like a fish and breathes with gills.

two days old

six days old

Frogs' eggs are covered with jelly. The jelly protects the eggs from enemies and keeps them warm.

In the picture above you can see the tadpole six days after hatching.

On the left you can see clumps of frogspawn in a pond. The parent frog leaves the spawn as soon as it is laid.

six weeks old

As the tadpole grows bigger, it starts to grow legs. The back legs appear first. The front legs are hidden by the gill flaps.

eight weeks old

After twelve weeks, the tadpole begins to look like a frog. The tail starts to shrink.

twelve weeks old

The adult frog has no tail and hops on its legs. It breathes with lungs and through its wet skin.

Most amphibians lay eggs which hatch into tadpoles. The tadpoles may look very different from their parents. They live in water and gradually change into adults. Then they leave the water and live on land. When they have grown up, they return to water to lay their eggs, called spawn.

adult frog

Frogs and toads

Frogs and toads are amphibians without tails. The largest is the goliath frog of Africa. It is 30 centimetres long. Frogs and toads walk or hop on land. In the water they swim with a breast stroke, like a human swimmer. Frogs have smoother skins than toads and longer legs.

Frogs and toads sing with croaks and grunts. This reed frog blows up its throat like a balloon when it sings.

The male midwife toad carries spawn from the female on his legs. He has to keep the spawn moist.

Tree frogs live in hot countries. They can climb well and jump from branch to branch. Their bright green colour matches their surroundings.

Newts and salamanders

Frogs and toads are amphibians without tails. Newts and salamanders are amphibians too, but they keep their tails when they are grown up. They look like lizards, but they have damp skins. When they run, they wiggle their bodies from side to side. Like other amphibians, they eat small animals.

Fire salamanders, like the one you can see below, live in Europe. People used to think that fire salamanders could walk through fire without being burned. This is not true.

The giant salamander comes from North America. It climbs trees and barks when alarmed.

The axolotl which you can see in the picture on the right is a salamander which never grows up. It spends its whole life as a tadpole.

When the time comes to lay eggs, newts gather in ponds. The male newts, like the one below, become brightly coloured.

Australian rock python

The Australian rock python curls around her eggs to protect them from enemies. She stays with them until they hatch.

REPTILES

Reptiles are animals which can spend all their lives on land. Their skins are covered with scales and are waterproof. Reptile eggs have a leathery skin and are laid on land. The eggs of some reptiles hatch inside the mother's body and the baby reptiles are born alive.

Millions of years ago the dinosaurs and other giant reptiles were the most important land animals.

The tuatara, which you can see in the picture above, is a very ancient reptile. It looks rather like a lizard. It lives on islands near New Zealand.

Reptiles are cold-blooded animals. Lizards warm their bodies by basking in the sun, like the one on the left. They can run faster when they are warm. At night lizards hide in holes or under stones to keep warm.

lizard

Lizards

Lizards are reptiles which usually have slender bodies and tails. The shingle-back lizard is fatter than other lizards. The frilled dragon runs on its back legs. The goanna has strong, curved claws but the gecko has special soles on its feet so that it can cling to walls. The legless lizard crawls like a snake.

legless lizard

leaf-tailed gecko

shingle-back lizard

spotted goanna

frilled dragon

Crocodiles

Crocodiles live near water and they can swim well. Some kinds of crocodiles live in the sea. Crocodiles usually eat fish but they can kill large animals by drowning them. They can grow up to eight metres in length. Crocodiles are now becoming very rare. Alligators and gharials are two kinds of crocodile.

American alligator

gharial

Siamese crocodile

Tortoises and turtles

Tortoises and turtles are reptiles with hard shells. Some kinds can pull their head and legs into the shell for safety. Tortoises live on land. Turtles live in water. Turtles' legs have developed into flippers which they use for swimming. They lay their eggs on land.

This giant tortoise is big enough to carry a boy on its back. Some giant tortoises live for over 150 years.

The green turtle lives in the sea. It eats a kind of grass which grows on the sea bed. Turtles come ashore to lay their eggs in the sand.

tur

tortoises

Tortoises grow very slowly and live for a very long time. They cannot walk very fast. They protect themselves by pulling their head and legs into their shell. Tortoises usually eat plants but they sometimes like to eat slugs and worms. Pet tortoises can be very big or very small.

terrapin

Terrapins are small turtles. They live in freshwater ponds and rivers. This red-eared terrapin has webbed feet and a tough shell.

Snakes

Snakes are reptiles without legs. They eat other animals and can open their mouths very wide to swallow large animals. Some snakes are poisonous. Others kill their victims by squeezing them to death.

Snakes are deaf and cannot hear the snake charmer's music. They sway in time to the man's movements.

This game of snakes and ladders shows some colourful snakes.

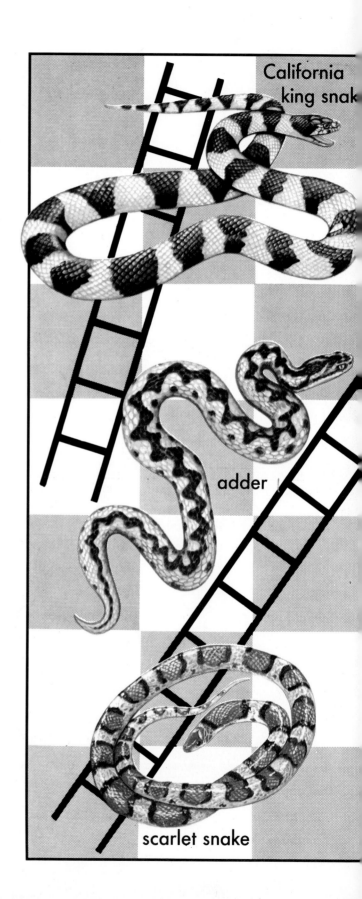

California king snake

adder

scarlet snake

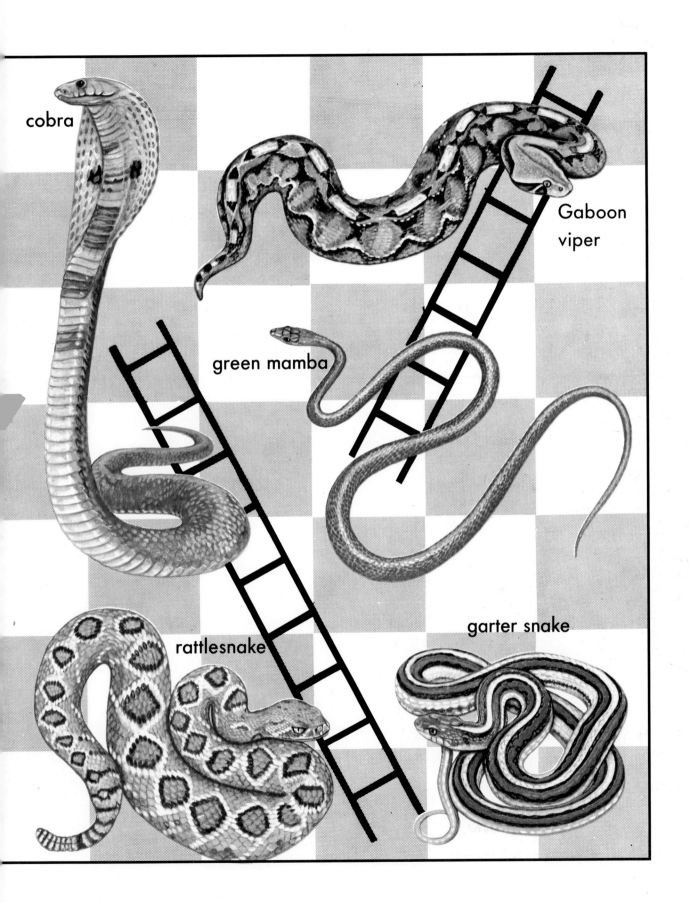

cobra

Gaboon
viper

green mamba

rattlesnake

garter snake

ATTACK AND DEFENCE

Cold-blooded animals have many different ways of harming their enemies. Bees and wasps sting to defend themselves. Poisonous snakes bite when they cannot escape. Other animals attack when they are looking for a meal. Some animals spread diseases when they suck blood.

Jellyfish can sting small animals which they then eat.

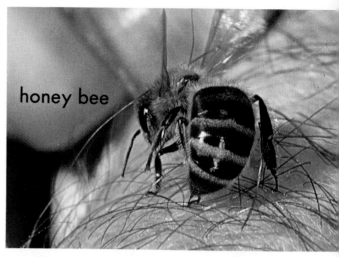

honey bee

The honey bee stings by injecting poison through a tube at the tip of its body.

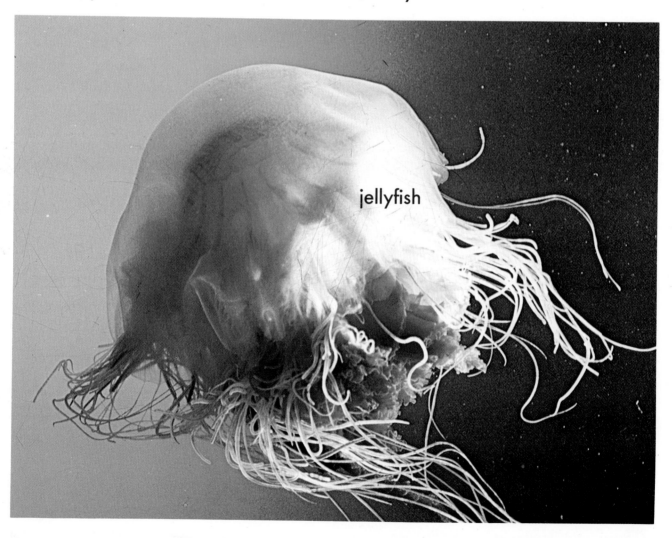

jellyfish

leech

Leeches, like the one in the picture above, cling to the skin of an animal and suck its blood.

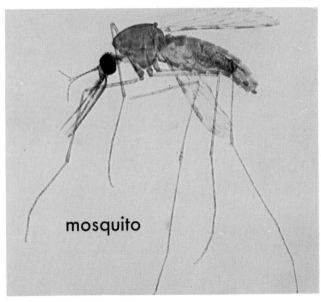

mosquito

piranha

Mosquitoes suck blood through a hollow tube. In hot countries they spread malaria and other diseases.

Piranhas are small fish. They attack large animals which wade or swim in the river.

Camouflage

Camouflage is a way of making things difficult to see. Animals are often camouflaged so that they cannot be seen by their enemies, or so that they can get near to their prey. The colours of the animals on this page match their background. The stick insect's shape also makes it difficult to see.

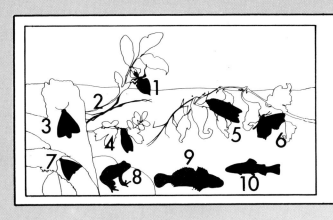

1 leaf insect   6 peacock butterfly
2 stick insect   7 carpet moth
3 goat moth   8 golden bell frog
4 cossid moth   9 bullhead fish
5 owlet moth   10 brown trout

DID YOU KNOW?

Many people keep cats and dogs as pets. These animals keep away rats and mice. In Borneo, some Chinese people keep pythons in their houses to scare away mice.

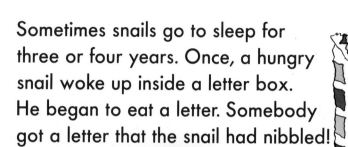

Sometimes snails go to sleep for three or four years. Once, a hungry snail woke up inside a letter box. He began to eat a letter. Somebody got a letter that the snail had nibbled!

One Friday, two snakes in the London Zoo were fighting over their dinner. Then one snake swallowed the other by mistake. Now the keepers watch very carefully to make sure it does not happen again. Keepers in zoos look after their animals very well. There is a story that they once fitted a snake with a glass eye!

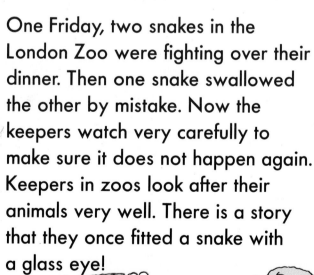

Tortoises eat leaves. Some leaves are poisonous, but the tortoises cannot taste the poisons very easily. This tortoise can taste poisons!

126

Warm-Blooded Animals

WARM-BLOODED ANIMALS

Mammals and birds are warm-blooded animals. Their bodies stay at the same temperature all the time. Mammals have fur and birds have feathers to help keep them warm. It is harder to keep warm in winter. We put on warm clothes. Many mammals grow thicker coats of fur.

shrew

hedgehog

mole

dormouse

squirrels

bats

squirrel

woodmouse

rabbit

rabbit

rabbits

badgers

129

BIRDS

Birds are the only animals in the world that have feathers. Their feathers help them to fly, and keep them warm and dry. Birds fly by beating their wings up and down. They use their tails to help them turn in the air. Their bodies are very light, which makes it easier for them to stay in the air.

The robin has a pointed beak for picking up insects and crumbs.

All birds lay eggs. The eggs have to be kept warm by the parent birds. When the chick is ready, it breaks through the eggshell. The parents look after the chick until it can fly.

Birds do not have hands. They use their beaks to hold things and build their nests. Birds do not have teeth either. They use their beaks for eating. You can tell what a bird eats by the shape of its beak.

The hawk has a hooked beak for tearing meat.

The hawfinch has a very strong, pointed beak for splitting seeds.

Eggs and baby birds are kept in a nest. There are many different kinds of nests. Some are cup-shaped and fixed to the twigs of a tree. Woodpeckers make holes in tree trunks. Some birds burrow in the ground. Many birds, like the mandarin duck, nest on the ground. The nest may be only a shallow pit lined with grass.

blackbird

weaver bird

woodpecker

teal

hummingbird

Tree birds

Many birds live in trees. Some build their nests among the branches. Others make holes in the trunk. Birds also find food in trees. They eat the fruit, flowers and leaves, or they catch insects that live on the leaves and in the bark.

The great spotted woodpecker nests in a hole in a tree trunk. It clings to the bark with sharp claws.

Brightly coloured parrots live in tropical forests. Their favourite foods are fruit, nuts and seeds.

Birds of paradise live in the hot forests of Australia and New Guinea. The males show off their beautiful colours from perches in the trees.

The crested pigeon on the right is guarding its chicks in a nest.
The chicks stay in the nest until they can fly. The parent birds take it in turns to bring them food.

ostrich

Ground birds

Some birds stay mostly on the ground. This is where they find their food. The turkey, which lives in North America, eats insects and berries on the ground. It sleeps in trees at night but cannot fly far. The ostrich has very small wings. It cannot fly at all. Ostriches have long legs and can run very fast.

turkey

These birds lived long ago. Now they have died out. They were large birds which could not fly.

dodo   moa   diatryma

The peacock is the male peafowl.
He opens his fan to attract the
peahen, the female. The feathers
grow from his back, not his tail.
Peahens do not have brightly
coloured feathers.

The kiwi lives in New Zealand. It has
tiny wings which are hidden under
its feathers. Kiwis come out at night
to search for worms.

Birds of prey

Birds that hunt and eat animals are called birds of prey. They have sharp claws to catch their prey, and hooked beaks to tear off the meat. Most birds of prey catch living animals. Vultures eat dead animals. Some birds of prey hunt in the daytime. Others hunt at night.

The osprey eats only fish. When it spots a fish, it dives feet-first into the water. It seizes the fish with its long sharp claws. Ospreys nest in high trees and cliffs.

The goshawk lives in forests where it hunts birds. It can move very quickly through the trees. This helps the hawk to chase its prey.

snowy owl

lemming

The snowy owl lives in the Arctic. Its white feathers help it to hide in the ice and snow. Most owls hunt at night, but the snowy owl hunts in the daytime. It mostly eats lemmings.

The barn owl hunts at night. Sometimes it hunts in the daytime as well when it has to find extra food for a hungry family of owlets.

Seabirds

Some seabirds, like the gannet, dive from high up to catch fish. Others dive from the surface of the water. Gulls, terns and fulmars stay near the coast. The wandering albatross flies out to sea to hunt.

puffin

Puffins nest in burrows in cliffs. They swim underwater to catch fish, and carry them back to the nest in their large beaks.

fulmar

common gull

kittiwakes

wandering albatross

shags

herring gull

Seabirds make their nests on cliffs and beaches. Kittiwakes make nests of seaweed on ledges high up the cliff. Shags nest lower down.

roseate tern

Arctic tern

gannet

Swans, ducks and geese

Ducks, geese and swans are called waterfowl. They have webbed feet for swimming and waterproof feathers to keep them dry in the water. Swans are the largest waterfowl. Ducks are the smallest. Swans and ducks often 'up-end' to find food underwater. Some ducks dive to the bottom of the pond to feed. Geese feed on land.

The shoveller uses its broad beak to sift food from mud.

Many geese nest in the far north. They fly south to warmer countries for the winter. Flocks of geese often make a V shape in the air. A flock of geese in the air is called a skein. A flock of geese on the ground is called a gaggle.

The merganser's beak has tiny hooks for holding slippery fish.

The mallard finds small insects and plants in ponds and streams.

Swans always land on water. They put out their feet like water-skis to help them slow down.
Ducks often flock together in winter. In the picture you can see mallard, pochard, pintail and others.

Long-legged birds

Some water birds do not swim very often. They use their long legs to wade through the water. They search for food in the water with their long necks and beaks. They like shallow water with plenty of plants. Lakes and swamps are good places for them to feed. The water is still. They can see food easily.

White storks build their nests on chimney tops. Some people make platforms for the storks. They think it is lucky to have a stork's nest on the house.

grey heron

Flamingoes live in large groups in the shallow water around lakes in warm countries. Flamingoes have longer necks than any other bird. They hold their beaks upside down in the water to feed. They sift tiny plants and animals out of the water and mud.

Cranes are the largest long-legged birds. Some cranes fly away to warm countries in the winter. Herons migrate as well. All the birds in this picture feed on fish and other tiny animals.

crane

stork

MAMMALS

There are 5,000 kinds of mammals. The mammals in this picture live in forests in South America. Some, like the monkeys and sloths, spend their time in the trees. Bats fly through the air. Other mammals, like the agouti, live in underground burrows. Giant otters swim in the rivers and eat fish. Jaguars often hunt tapirs, as well as sloths and monkeys.

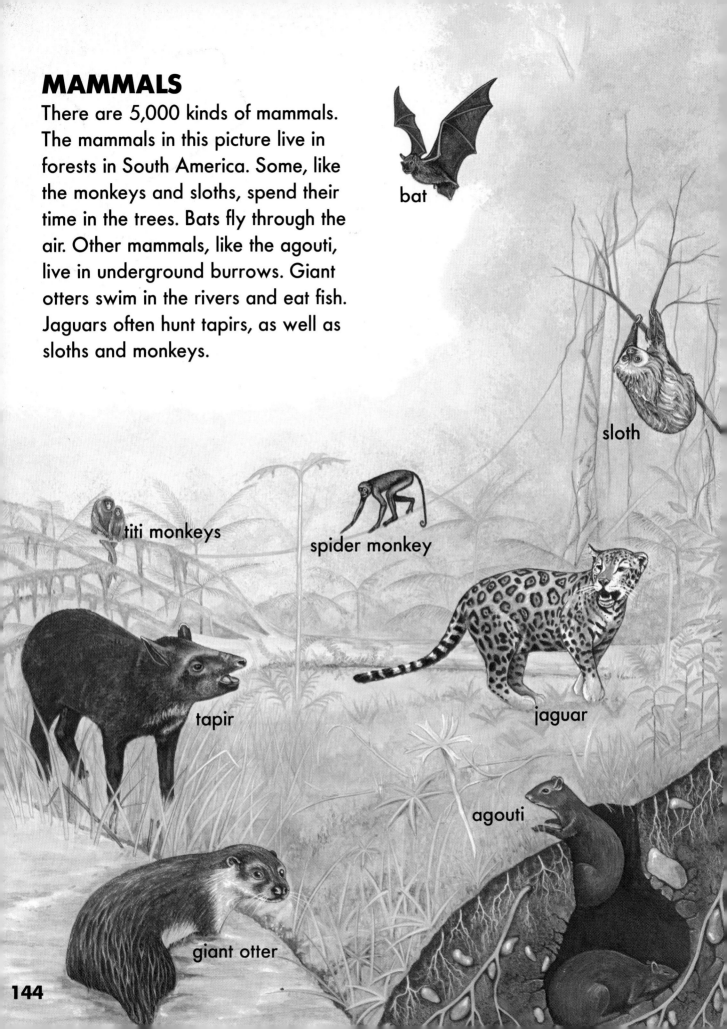

bat

sloth

titi monkeys

spider monkey

jaguar

tapir

agouti

giant otter

All baby mammals feed on milk from their mother's body. No other animals feed their babies this way. Some baby mammals, like kittens and puppies, are helpless when they are first born. Their mothers keep them warm. Other baby mammals, like foals and piglets, can run about when they are only a few hours old.

duck-billed platypus

Only two kinds of mammals lay eggs. All other mammals give birth to baby mammals. The duck-billed platypus and the echidna lay eggs. They both live in Australia and New Guinea.

koalas

Some mammals keep their newborn babies in a pouch. These mammals are called marsupials. The koala is a marsupial. A baby koala is only two centimetres long when it is born.

Pouched mammals

Pouched mammals are called marsupials. They live mainly in Australia. Kangaroos, wallabies, koalas and many other marsupials live there. Opossums live in America. Many marsupials look like other kinds of mammals. The koala looks like a small bear. There are also marsupial moles and marsupial rats.

When the baby kangaroo is born it is only a few centimetres long. It crawls through its mother's fur and into her pouch. It stays there until it has grown much larger.

Bilbys live in burrows as rabbits do. They come out only at night to eat insects. They are sometimes called rabbit bandicoots.

Kangaroos hop with both legs together. They leap as far and as high as athletes.

The scrub wallaby is a small kangaroo that can hop very fast.

147

Monkeys and apes

Monkeys and apes nearly all live in forests, where they climb the trees. Their hands and feet are good at grasping the branches. There are monkeys in America that can hang by their tails. Baboons live on the ground, but they climb trees when they are frightened. Monkeys eat mainly leaves and fruit.

mandrill

olive baboon

howler monkey

bonnet monkey

marmoset

The four kinds of ape are the orang-utan, the gibbon, the gorilla and the chimpanzee.

Apes do not have tails. Gibbons and orang-utans swing through the trees by their arms. Gorillas and chimpanzees live mainly on the ground. Apes are very intelligent.

gorilla

chimpanzee

gibbon

orang-utan

GNAWING ANIMALS

Many mammals gnaw their food. These mammals are called rodents. The most common rodents are rats, mice and voles.

Rodents have long front teeth for gnawing. Their teeth are always sharp and they grow as fast as they wear down. They are used to chew tough food such as nuts and roots.

Rabbits and hares are gnawing animals but they are not rodents. They have an extra pair of front teeth in their upper jaws which rodents do not have.

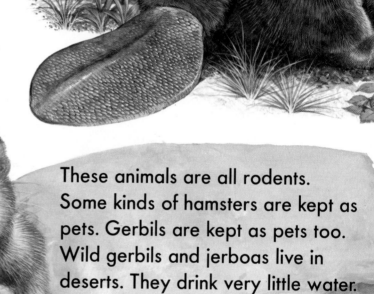

hamster

jerboa

These animals are all rodents. Some kinds of hamsters are kept as pets. Gerbils are kept as pets too. Wild gerbils and jerboas live in deserts. They drink very little water.

gerbil

beaver

A beaver can cut down trees with its teeth. It eats the bark and uses the trunk and branches to dam a river. A pond is formed behind the dam where the beaver builds its home with twigs and branches. Its home is called a lodge.

Squirrels are rodents. They eat nuts, acorns and berries with their sharp teeth. Most squirrels live in trees. They are good climbers and can jump from branch to branch. They have bushy tails which help them to balance.

Rats and mice

There are many different kinds of rats and mice. Most of them are harmless but a few are pests. Animals become pests when they live in huge numbers and cause damage. Rats and mice eat our crops and spread diseases.
Even when they are pests we hardly ever see them. They live in burrows and are very shy.

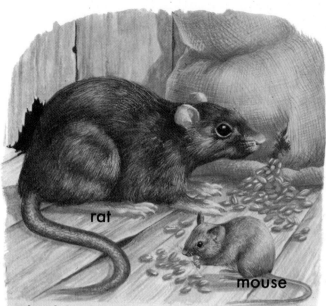

rat

mouse

The black rat and the house mouse are pests which live in houses and barns. They eat stores of grain and other food.

The harvest mouse builds a nest of grass above the ground. The nest is fixed to the plant stems. A favourite home is in fields of wheat.

Rabbits and hares

Rabbits and hares have long front teeth but they are not rodents. They have long ears, long legs and short tails. Rabbits live in burrows and their babies are born blind. Hares do not burrow. Their babies are born with their eyes open.

jack rabbit

Arctic hare

Rabbits and hares lose body heat through their ears. The American jack rabbit lives in the desert. It has extra long ears which help it to keep cool. The Arctic hare has small ears so it does not lose heat in the cold Arctic air.

rabbits

SEA MAMMALS

Seals, sealions and walruses are mammals which live in the sea. They come ashore to have their babies and to rest. They have flippers for swimming but are clumsy on land. Sealions and walruses can bound along the ground quite fast by tucking up their back flippers.

On the right are some walruses. They use their tusks to dig for food.

The picture below shows a baby grey seal, called a pup, with its mother. The pup goes to sea by itself when it is only three weeks old.

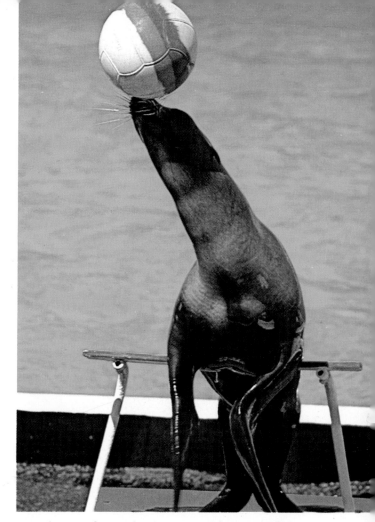

The diver below is wearing flippers. They help him to swim as easily as the sealion. The diver has to take his air supply with him.

Seals and sealions are clever. They can be taught tricks. This sealion has learned to balance a ball on its nose.

Whales

Whales spend their whole lives in water. They cannot come ashore. Dolphins and porpoises are small whales. Whales swim with their tails, which have two paddles called flukes. Their nostrils are on top of their heads. They are called blowholes. Blue whales eat shrimps. Other whales eat mainly fish.

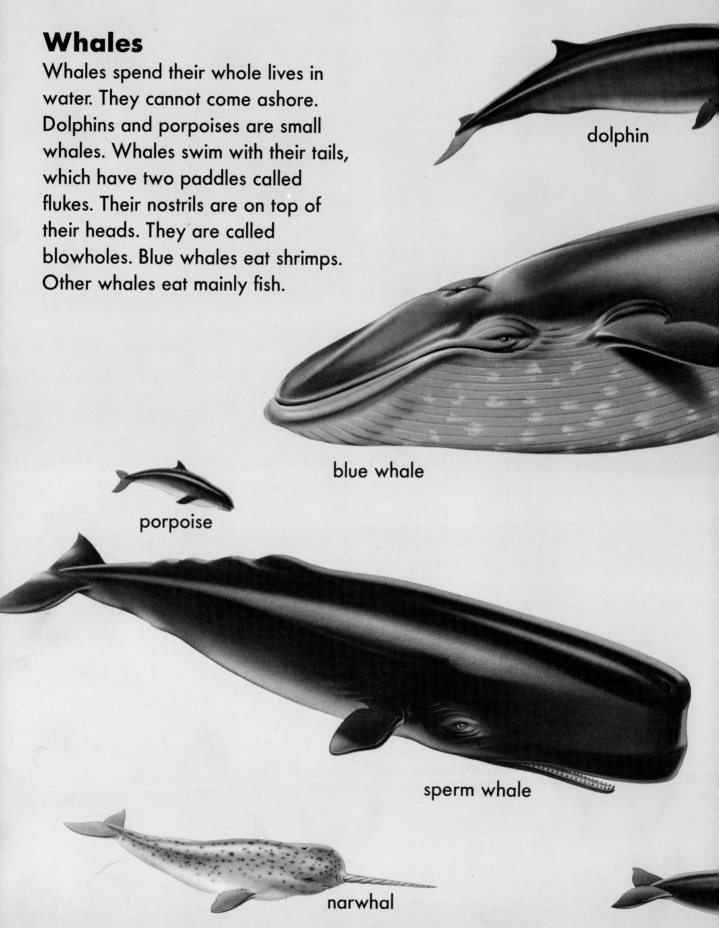

dolphin

blue whale

porpoise

sperm whale

narwhal

Greenland whale

killer whale

pilot whale

MEAT-EATERS

Carnivores are hunting animals that eat meat. They are strong and run fast to catch other animals, called prey. Carnivores have sharp teeth for killing their prey. Cats, dogs, mongooses and weasels are all carnivores. Some carnivores, like tigers, are very large and sometimes kill people.

The weasel is a small carnivore, but it is very fierce. It can kill animals as big as a rabbit.

The wild cat in the big picture is showing four long, pointed teeth. These teeth are called canines, or fangs. They are for stabbing and killing the wild cat's prey.

The mongoose is famous for killing poisonous snakes, like this cobra. It moves so fast that the snake does not have time to bite.

Although the giant panda is a carnivore it eats mainly plants. Its favourite food is bamboo. Giant pandas live in China.

leopard

prey

Leopards live in Africa and Asia. They are so strong that they can climb a tree with their prey. They leave the prey in the branches of the tree so that other animals do not steal it. This leopard has killed a gazelle.

The cat family

There are about 40 kinds of wild cats. Most of them are not much bigger than pet cats. Five kinds of cats are known as 'The Big Cats'. They are the lion, tiger, leopard, jaguar and snow leopard.

Cats usually hunt alone. They wait patiently for their prey, or creep towards it and pounce suddenly.

Babies of big cats are called cubs. The jaguar cubs, above, are from South America. Baby cats learn to hunt by playing together.

Manx

tabby

Siamese

Lion families are called prides. A pride is led by a male lion, who has a mane of fur. In the picture above you can see a lioness and her cubs. Lionesses do most of the hunting for the pride. They catch zebra and other large animals.

There are many kinds of pet cats. The tabby cat looks like the African wild cat that lived thousands of years ago. The Siamese cat was once kept in temples in Siam, now called Thailand. The Manx cat has long back legs but no tail.

Dogs and bears

Dogs and bears are carnivores. They are related to each other but their habits are different. Bears are heavy animals. They walk slowly on the soles of their feet. Dogs walk on their toes. They are good runners and can travel long distances without getting tired. Dogs are hunters. In the wild they often live in groups called packs.

fox

There are many breeds of dogs. Some dogs are kept as pets, but others have to work for their living. This bouvier from Belgium is used for herding cattle.

Bears are carnivores but most bears eat mainly berries and leaves. They have long claws and small bears can climb trees. Bears live alone and sleep through the winter. The polar bear lives in the Arctic, and can swim well. Polar bears are hunters. They eat both fish and seals.

The fox is one of the dog family which hunts alone. It comes out at night to look for mice to eat.

polar bear

This brown bear is feeding her cubs. The cubs are born in her winter den and come out with her in the spring. They follow her and she teaches them how to find food.

Hoofed mammals

A hoof is a very large toenail.
Animals with hoofs stand on tiptoes.
Their weight rests on their hoofs.

There are many kinds of hoofed
animals. Some, like the American
bison and the African wildebeest,
live in huge herds. All hoofed
animals are plant-eaters.

Mouse deer are the smallest kind of
hoofed animal. They are only
30 centimetres tall. They live in
forests in Africa and Asia, and come
out to feed at night.

Giraffes grow to nearly six metres
tall. They live on the plains of Africa.
They can eat leaves from the highest
branches.

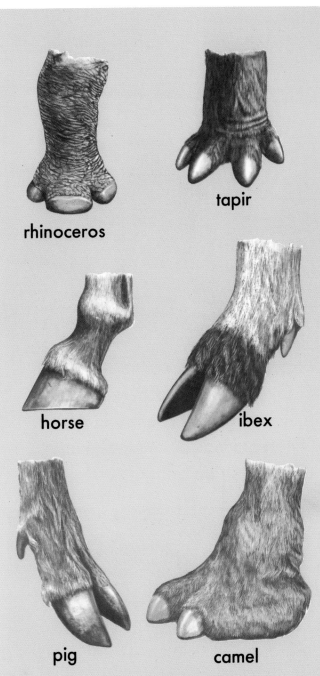

rhinoceros

tapir

horse

ibex

pig

camel

There are two kinds of hoofed animal. One kind has an even number of toes. The other kind has an odd number. Animals that have two toes are called cloven-hoofed.

Horses and ponies

Horses have only one hoof on each leg. The hoofs of domestic horses are protected by steel horseshoes. The horseshoes are put on by a blacksmith.

The zebra is a kind of wild horse. It lives in grassy country in Africa. Different kinds of zebras have different stripe patterns.

This odd-looking animal is a zedonk. One of its parents is a zebra. The other is a donkey.

Wild horses once lived in Europe and Asia. They were the ancestors of all the domestic horses that we know today. There are very few really wild horses left. Most of the horses that now live in the wild were once domestic animals. The white horses in the picture on the right used to be domesticated. Now they run free in the Camargue in the south of France.

Ponies are small horses. They often live in wild places and they are good for riding.

Deer and antelopes

Deer and antelopes are cloven-hoofed animals. Deer have antlers but antelopes have horns. Antlers are made of bone. Deer shed their antlers and grow new ones each year. The antlers of a red deer get bigger as it grows older. Only male deer have antlers, except for reindeer. Both male and female reindeer have antlers.

female red deer

antlers

moose

male
red deer

eland

horns

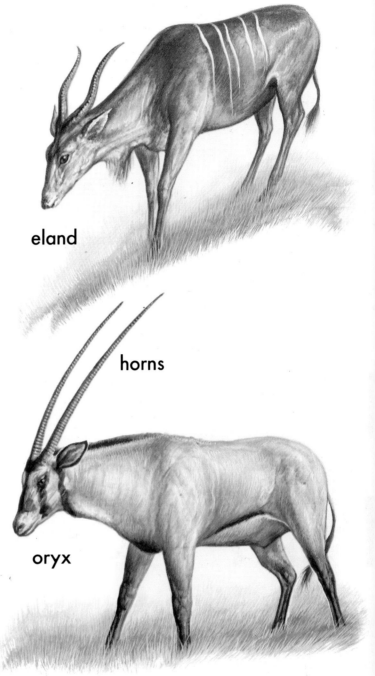

oryx

—Thompson's
gazelles

All antelopes have horns like those
of goats and cattle. Both males and
females have horns. Most antelopes
live in Africa but there are some in
Asia. The oryx lives in deserts and
the gazelle lives on grassy plains.
The eland is the largest antelope in
the world.

Cattle, sheep and goats

These cloven-hoofed animals are important because they provide us with meat, milk and wool. Prehistoric people used to hunt wild cattle, sheep and goats. Now these animals are domesticated and live on farms.

Goats, like the one on the right, eat almost anything. They can even climb trees to eat the leaves and bark. The male goat has a beard and is called a billy goat.

Kerryhill

Toggenburg

British Alpine

British Saarinen

Hampshire

Suffolk

Merino ram

All these domestic animals eat grass. Sheep are farmed for wool and meat. Some cows are kept for milk, others for meat.

Bison are a kind of wild ox. They live on the American prairies. They were once hunted for their meat.

Highland

Charolais

Aberdeen Angus

Jersey

Friesian

Giant mammals

These are the biggest animals that live on land. The largest animal is the African elephant. It is more than three metres high and weighs more than ten tonnes. All these animals eat plants. Elephants eat leaves and bark too. They need a huge amount of food every day.

Rhinoceroses can be dangerous. They can run very fast. Sometimes they charge at people or cars.

The hippopotamus lives in rivers and swamps in Africa. It spends most of its time in the water but comes ashore at night to feed. It eats mainly grass.

Indian elephants have smaller ears and tusks than African elephants. They have been tamed for hundreds of years. They lift tree trunks, and are ridden in parades.

anteaters

HOW ANIMALS LIVE

There are many kinds of animals in the world. They all have different ways of finding food and looking after their babies. They live in different places and eat different things. Some animals behave in unusual ways. All the animals on this page are rather strange and have some odd habits.

There are three kinds of anteaters in South America. The ones above are giant anteaters. They eat insects by licking them up with their long sticky tongues. Female anteaters carry their babies on their back. They carry them around until the babies are quite big, as you can see in the picture above.

The gerenuk stands on its back legs to eat the leaves on high branches.

muskoxen

174

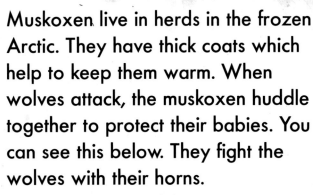

Muskoxen live in herds in the frozen Arctic. They have thick coats which help to keep them warm. When wolves attack, the muskoxen huddle together to protect their babies. You can see this below. They fight the wolves with their horns.

The mole lives in underground tunnels where it finds worms to eat.

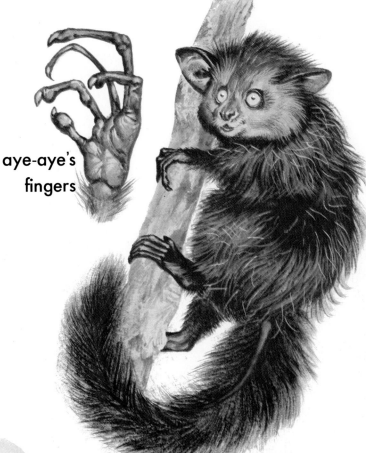

aye-aye's fingers

The aye-aye uses its long fingers to find insects that live in wood.

Animals that help us

People's lives would be very different without domestic animals. Animals have been used for thousands of years to help with heavy work. They are used mainly for pulling loads and for riding.

Today, tractors and trucks are used for these jobs, but animals still work in some countries.

Sheepdogs are used to herd sheep. The shepherd whistles and calls to the dog to tell it what to do.

Reindeer pull sledges in the Arctic. They can travel about 60 kilometres in a day.

Most farmers today use tractors to pull the plough. You can still sometimes see horses being used. The ploughman has to be very skilled.

In some countries, oxen are used for ploughing, and for pulling carts. Can you see the wooden yoke that joins the oxen to the cart?

Camels are used for carrying people and goods in the desert. They can go for days without drinking and can work in the hot sun. Camels are also used for ploughing.

Animals of the night

All these animals come out at night. They spend the day in burrows, in nests or in holes in trees. We may sometimes see them in the evening or lit up by car headlights at night. Night animals usually find their way by scent or by hearing. The owl can see well in the dark.

pipistrell

dormouse

woodmouse

badger

Animal weapons

Animals have many ways of defending themselves. They usually run away from danger, but they sometimes have to fight. Antelopes and rhinoceroses use their horns. Elephants use their tusks. Horses kick with their hoofs. The animals on these pages have some unusual ways of defending themselves.

When kangaroos fight, they hug each other and kick with their back legs. A kick from a kangaroo could kill a man.

This opossum is pretending to be dead. The dog does not like dead animals and leaves it alone.

Llamas live in the Andes mountains. They spit when they are angry.

The porcupine's spines are like a hedgehog's but they are longer. They are called quills and they stick into the face of an attacker.

Skunks defend themselves from their enemies by squirting a horrid-smelling liquid.

Armadillos are protected by bony armour. This one has rolled into a ball for extra safety.

Animal camouflage

Many animals hide to protect themselves. The best way to hide is to keep very still, but it helps to have colours that match the surrounding colours. Some cold-blooded animals can even change colour. The animals shown here have colours and patterns that make them hard to see.

The nightjar nests on the ground. Its colour makes it almost impossible to see.

Stone curlews hunt for insects at night. In the day they sit on their nests. The colours of their feathers help them to hide on the ground.

The cheetah's spots break up the outline of its body so that it is difficult to see in the grass.

In the spring, ptarmigan have brown feathers. They cannot be seen when they are sitting on their nests.

In the winter, ptarmigan grow white feathers. You can see them in the picture on the left.

Animals in danger

Every year more animals are in danger of becoming extinct. Some are hunted for their fur or because they eat our crops. Other animals have nowhere to live because the forests are being cut down so that the land can be turned into farms.

Some animals only survive in special reserves. The European bison that you can see on the right are found only in one forest in Poland.

European bison

Wild asses are hunted for their meat. Only a few now live in the middle of the desert.

The bald eagle is now becoming rare. It is shot and poisoned by farmers to protect their animals.

orang-utan

The condor is the world's largest flying bird but farmers kill it to protect their animals.

The forests of Borneo and Sumatra are being cut down. There is nowhere for the orang-utan to live.

Extinct animals

Many animals will never be seen again. They have become extinct because they were hunted until none were left.

Steller's seacow lived in the Arctic Ocean. It became extinct only a few years after it had been discovered by explorers.

Steller's seacow

great auk

The last great auk was seen in Iceland 100 years ago. Great auks could not fly and they were easily killed by sailors for food.

The Tasmanian wolf was hunted because it killed sheep. It has not been seen for many years.

Tasmanian wolf

186

giant aurochs

The giant aurochs once lived in Europe. They are the ancestors of our cattle.

quagga

Herds of quaggas lived in South Africa. They were hunted for meat and became extinct 100 years ago.

DID YOU KNOW?

This Californian sea otter is about to eat its dinner. It uses its chest as a table. Then it breaks open tasty crabs and sea-urchins with a small rock.

There are more cows living in France than in any of the countries nearby!

Polar bears live in snowy and icy lands around the Arctic. They can travel very fast on the ice, up to 15 kilometres an hour. Polar bears have hairy feet which help them to keep a firm grip on the ice.

Moles tunnel through the ground at night. They can tunnel as much as 75 metres during one night.

Index